Books by Era Zistel

Treasury of Cat Stories
Golden Book of Cat Stories
Golden Book of Dog Stories
Orphan
The Good Year
Wintertime Cat
The Gentle People
Thistle
The Dangerous Year
Hi Fella
Good Companions

Good
Companions

Good

Companions

ERA ZISTEL

LITTLE, BROWN AND COMPANY
BOSTON – TORONTO

FIRST EDITION

LIBRARY OF CONGRESS CATALOGING IN PUBLICATION DATA
Zistel, Era.
Good companions.
I.   Animals, Legends and stories of.   I.   Title.
QL791.Z52   818'.5407   79–26780
ISBN 0–316–98797–6

MV

Designed by Susan Windheim

Published simultaneously in Canada
by Little, Brown & Company (Canada) Limited

PRINTED IN THE UNITED STATES OF AMERICA

*For my good friend
Isabelle Griffis*

Good Companions

O THE EVENTS in our lives occur entirely by chance? Was it only by accident that I glanced out the window one day at what seemed like just the wrong moment? Or had my doing so been planned by fate, or destiny, or whatever one might wish to call the supervisory force that, viewed from afar, runs the universe in a fairly orderly fashion?

A stray cat was walking through the yard. If I had glanced out a moment earlier it would not yet have arrived. A moment later, it would have been gone. But I chose to look out the window just when it was *there*, a scraggly gray cat with three white paws, the fourth not white because that part of the paw was missing. It limped a few more steps, then stopped and waited, as if sensing my presence at the window and knowing quite well what would follow.

What followed was routine. As I had any number of times before, I piled food on a plate, went outside, and put the plate down on the ground. But, I told myself, this time would be different. This time I would not make friends. I already had too many cats, most of them acquired in much the same way. Another was definitely not welcome. So I put down the plate and at once walked away, without even a glance around to see whether the cat was still there. However, back in the house I did look through the window again, to make sure the food wasn't going to waste. It wasn't.

The next afternoon at about the same time, the cat was in the yard again, not passing through, but just sitting where I had placed the food the day before. Again I brought out a plate and put it down and walked away, giving him not a word of greeting or even a glance, making it clear, I thought, that his presence was tolerated, but not particularly appreciated.

The third day when he saw me with the plate he came limping over to meet me, but, unlike those others who preceded him, he did not follow through with the usual feline blandishments of sinuating against my legs, or rising on his hind legs to nudge against the hand that offered sustenance. Instead, he simply stood waiting for me to put the plate down, then continued to wait until I left before he started eating. It was almost as if he were assuring me that he would accept the relationship on my terms; he would ask from me nothing more than the assuaging of his hunger.

Day after day I took the food out and put it down. Day after day he came and ate, and finally he no longer departed after eating, but sat in the yard, just sat, and whenever I appeared he immediately stood up, as if paying homage to royalty. Still I spoke no word, until one day when I went out with the food and he didn't seem to be visible I said, only to myself, "Well, where is he?" and at once he was standing next to me, as if materialized out of thin air, to respond to my question with a rusty little squeak that sounded as if his voice hadn't been used in a long time. So he acquired a name. The next day I said, "Hi, Squeak," and that was that. As everyone knows, once you give an animal a name you have capitulated.

Nevertheless, our relationship remained satisfactorily tenuous. His only obligation was to eat, mine only to provide the food. But of course such an arrangement was too perfect to last. One day he had had time for only one bite before two neighborhood dogs charged into the yard. He fled in terror, and before I could chase them away they gulped down his dinner. The next day the same thing happened, and it was clear that Squeak would have to be fed elsewhere or starve.

I did some searching and eventually found an old piece of siding that seemed suitable, cut it to length, affixed braces, and nailed it to the frame of the kitchen window. There, out of reach of the dogs, Squeak could eat in peace. But there, it turned out, he could also peer through the window to watch the comings and goings in the kitchen, and next to eating this became his favorite pastime. Hour after hour he sat on the shelf on the other side of the glass, sometimes dozing, but always remaining alert enough to rise and pay homage whenever I passed by, which I found so disconcerting that I began staying out of the kitchen as much as possible.

Then with the coming of autumn an extraordinary thing happened. After the birds and squirrels returned from their summer vacations in the woods, I put out dry bread and suet for them as usual, but the impudent chickadees soon found they much preferred the cat food I served to Squeak. At feeding time they fluttered around his shelf waiting for me to bring it out and, to my utter amazement, swooped down to join him while he ate. Couldn't they see that he was a cat? Showing absolutely no fear, they pecked at the food on one side of the plate while he ate on the other side, paying little attention to them unless one fluttered too close around his head. Then sometimes he raised a paw to deliver an impatient swat.

It wasn't long before a squirrel — or, since I couldn't tell them apart, perhaps several squirrels — took note of Squeak's tolerance and darted in every once in a while to grab a bite. And in time I got so used to seeing this strange assemblage outside the kitchen window that it no longer seemed remarkable. I simply doubled Squeak's rations, so that his forbearance would not condemn him to go hungry.

His attachment to the shelf became worrisome. He would hop off it to take care of certain necessities, which involved traveling a considerable distance so as not to contaminate the area around the house, then hurry back to leap up and resume the guarding of this, his sole property. Even during the night he was there, somehow managing to curl up on the narrow ledge without falling off. When the heavy rains of autumn came he still squatted, hunched up, soaking wet, looking so miserable that my feelings alternated between pity and fury with him for being so possessive.

At last I went on another hunt for lumber and made a roof over the shelf, a ramshackle affair that certainly did nothing to improve the appearance of the house, but it served its purpose. The shelf stayed dry, and Squeak looked a lot more comfortable, at least until the weather turned cold.

When the first snow fell I couldn't stand watching him shiver and tried to coax him into the house. To all my pleading he responded with only the flick of an ear and a slight adjustment of position. Finally I reached up, plucked him off the shelf, and carried him indoors. His body stiffened with fear, but he didn't scratch or bite or protest in any way until I put him down on the floor. Then his sphincter muscles let go, to leave dribbles and deposits all over as he howled and raced around and leaped against the walls in wild efforts to escape. Far from being a refuge, the house was for him a huge trap. Reluctantly I opened the door to let him out again.

A few days later fierce winds of another storm put a deep pile of snow on the shelf. I brushed it off and gave him his food, and he and the chickadees ate as usual. But as soon as the plate was empty, he hopped down from the shelf, and this time he did not return. The next morning the snow on the ground revealed that he had found another place to live, or at least sleep. A line of tracks, the tracks of a cat, straight as if drawn by a ruler, the indentations of the back paws precisely in those made by the front paws, led to the old barn behind the house, long abandoned after the goats were moved to a new barn nearby. Some hay still remained in the old stalls, and in one mound Squeak had hollowed out a bowl to lie in. This was to be his home for the winter, a poor counterfeit of the box near the stove that he might have enjoyed, but at least a shelter of sorts from the cold winds and snow.

The trouble was that he still felt obligated to pay his respects to me. While he was on the shelf he had always stood at attention when he saw me in the kitchen. Now whenever he heard me emerge from the house he had to leave his nest in the barn and trek through the snow, just to stand nearby while I took care of whatever chore had brought me out of doors. This distracted me so, especially late at night when I took out food for the birds to find in the morning, that I tried to sneak out, opening and closing the door behind me as cautiously as a thief, but he always heard me anyway. Soon there was a well-worn path in the snow, leading from the barn to the house and back again, and the peculiar thing about this path was that it changed only in growing deeper. Each time he went back and forth his feet were placed in exactly the same indentations, so that the line remained unaltered, and there was no way of telling which way he had traveled last, out of the barn or into it. But there was no doubt as to his whereabouts whenever I was outside, and his constancy bothered me so that I figured out all sorts of ways to combine chores, sometimes carrying almost impossible loads, so as to reduce the number of trips he'd have to make.

At last winter came to an end. The snow melted, the air warmed, and, mostly as an excuse to stay out of doors, I decided that before the goats moved in to spend the summer there, I would clean up the pasture, an acre of cleared land down the hill, a few hundred feet from the house. Each afternoon I spent an hour or so raking leaves and picking up fallen branches to put them on a pile, and in a few days I noticed that I never seemed to be alone. Squeak was always there, too, not exactly with me, but somewhere in the vicinity, sitting on a rock or a knoll or a log, gravely watching me work. Then I noticed that whenever I walked down the hill to the pasture he was also walking down the hill, not with me, but just sort of going in the same direction. And finally, near the usual time for me to start out, I'd see him sitting in the path, waiting, and as soon as I left the house he would start walking ahead, solemnly leading the way. So began a strange relationship that actually brought about a change in my life.

Never was land more meticulously tidied than that acre of pasture. When even the smallest twigs had been picked up and put in a neat pile and there was no more reason at all for me to go down the hill, I made the daily trip anyway because Squeak was always waiting. In the middle of the pasture there was a big flat rock, almost ten feet in diameter and as smooth as a polished tabletop. Since I had nothing else to do, I'd go and sit on this rock, and after several days Squeak walked briskly ahead of me, hopped on the rock, and stood waiting for me. We'd sit side by side, he purring with eyes half-closed, I with head tilted back, gazing at the blue sky and the towering old maples circling the pasture, and that was the first lesson I learned from him: how to relax. For maybe half an hour of not moving, not thinking, I would float on tranquillity until roused, perhaps by the anxious flutterings and urgent cries of a thrush teaching her timid fledgling to fly. Then reluctantly I'd leave our rock and return to the world, with Squeak always following.

The grass in the pasture grew tall. It was past time for the goats to enjoy grazing there. I had misgivings about disappointing Squeak, but he seemed to understand. From a little way off he watched me take the goats down the hill in the morning and watched again when they returned at sundown. Then he sat in the middle of the path to remind me, so we continued having our conferences, as I came to call them, only at a different and actually more pleasant hour, when the light had softened, and from treetops on all sides the song of the thrushes rang out like chimes striking the hour.

Each day I retrieved a log from the brush pile and on our return trip carried it up the hill for a fire to ward off the mountain chill in the evening. Finally in late summer there were no logs left, only small branches and twigs, and I had to look for firewood elsewhere, which necessitated a relocation of our conferences.

Again Squeak seemed to understand. After only a few trips in a different direction, he gave up sitting in the path to the pasture and waited instead near the brook in back of the house. A little way off on the other side of it, a stand of old trees that has always been referred to as the woodlot offered enough fallen branches and trunks to last an entire winter. We crossed the brook on stepping-stones, then threaded our way among the trees until we came upon a suitable log. Little sunlight filtered through the heavy foliage, but somewhere nearby Squeak would find a spot to bask in while I cut the log and loaded the pieces on the small cart I'd brought along. Then we'd search out a rock for our conference. Nowhere did we find one to compare with the big smooth slab in the pasture, but we adjusted to smaller ones that were not too bumpy.

Summer came to an end. The air cooled, and leaves falling from the trees rustled continuously around us, but sometimes above the rustling we would hear small feet ploughing through, and our heads would turn in unison, to catch sight of a passing chipmunk or squirrel, or perhaps nothing at all. Once, we became aware of a furtive disturbance directly in front of us, near my feet. Leaves shifted and rose as if something underneath were pushing them, and as we stared at the spot a small head emerged, tiny nose twitching to test the air, eyes no bigger than pinheads darting about to check the terrain, ears proportionately as big as an elephant's alert for any sound. A white-footed deer mouse was coming out of its tunnel for a look around. Neither Squeak nor I stirred, so no movement betrayed our presence, but the beady eyes must have brought us into focus, two living creatures, one enormous, towering overhead. Instantly the head withdrew, the leaves settled, and the appearance of the mouse became only something we might have imagined. I chuckled, and Squeak looked up at me.

"You can't be a cat," I said. "What are you, then? Who are you?"

One day we heard strange sounds in the distance, like the creaking of innumerable wagon wheels, and a broad, undulating river appeared in the sky. It traveled swiftly toward us, slowed down just overhead, widened like a stream entering a pond, then with a deafening crescendo of the creaking and a mighty roar of wings it descended. The tree around us turned black, with shifting bodies covering all the branches. The banks of the brook turned black as hundreds of birds dipped their beaks into the water. For a second all the creaking stopped, and the sudden silence was almost terrifying. Then with a mighty surge of wings those at the brook rose like a tidal wave, and a descending wave from the trees replaced them. Again the air became almost solid with cries that beat against the ears, throbbed in the head, threatened to obliterate identity. And again there was silence. It was as if we were caught in the bloodstream of a giant, listening to the ebb and flow of its pulse. Then with a tremendous beating of wings the birds were all at once sucked up from the ground, snatched off the trees, whirled in a screaming vortex, and swept away. The river flowed south, the cries died away in the distance, and the air thinned by the absence of sound seemed almost hard to breathe. But soon there were more cries far to the north, faint and lonely, and after a while stragglers appeared. Widely separated, belonging not even to each other, they went on without stopping to rest or drink, slipping like spent arrows into the empty sky to the south. Why had they fallen behind? Were they doomed?

The migration of the blackbirds was a winter warning. The red and gold leaves turned brown. The temperature dropped to almost freezing, and strong north winds increased the chill. Because of the fuel shortage, I was, like many other people, trying to rely on burning logs in the stove for heat, and that meant spending considerably more time in the woods. Squeak sat hunched up while I cut and loaded the day's supply, and when we had our conference, with the rock's coldness even making me shiver, he at last dared to put his forepaws on my lap, while I encircled him with an arm to warm him.

The first snow fell. I tried sneaking out of the house and into the woods without him, but he always heard the sound of the cart and hurried out of the barn to catch up with me. More snow fell, and more, until it was so deep that he had to wait for me to go ahead and break trail, then follow in my tracks. All the rocks were buried. There was nothing to sit on but snow, and I had the double discomfort of seeing him hunched on it, shivering, then sitting on it myself to hold him and try to warm him.

At long last it occurred to me that we might have something other than snow to sit on, and I took along a heavy burlap bag to spread near the log I was cutting. He sniffed at it suspiciously the first day, not giving it his trust until I sat on it. But after that he went to it as soon as it was put down, and enjoyed it so much that he even did a bit of grooming, washing his face and his belly and giving his spraddled legs a few licks. When the logs had been cut and loaded on the cart I'd join him, and on sunny days with no wind blowing, with the snow sparkling and the great trees rising all around us like the pillars of a cathedral, and no sound anywhere but the chattering of a woodpecker, our conferences were actually so pleasant that I almost hated to leave.

"But what if a hunter or a skier came this way?" I said. "What would he think, seeing a human and a cat huddled together in the middle of the woods like this, sitting on a burlap bag in the snow?"

It was ludicrous, of course. Yet it was a precious interval of peace, in which nothing mattered but the contentment of simply being.

He had learned the word *home* and as soon as it was spoken would get to his feet. I'd fold the burlap bag and put it on top of the logs on the cart, and he would lead the way back on the path we had made coming in through the snow. Sometimes the load on the cart would slip, and I'd have to stop to make adjustments. He always stopped, too, and stood by until I was ready to go on. Or I'd lose my footing and fall. The first time he came hurrying back to stand beside me as I lay on the snow I thought it was only coincidence. Cats are not supposed to be solicitous. But it happened again and again, and always he seemed reassured when I laughed, as if he knew that meant I was not hurt. And once more I'd have the uncanny feeling that he was something other than a cat.

At home his living conditions worsened. The abandoned barn where he chose to sleep was gradually falling apart. Snow sifted through a hole in the roof, and I feared high winds or a very heavy snowfall might send the whole building crashing down on him. Somehow he had to be persuaded to live elsewhere.

The new barn where the goats resided was divided by a wall into two sections. The stalls in which they spent most of their time during the winter months were on one side. The other side contained their hay, and also sheltered me from the wind when I cut into smaller chunks the logs I had brought in from the woods. Certainly this would be a much more comfortable home for Squeak, if only he could be persuaded to accept it.

I hollowed out a nest in the hay, and as soon as he had finished his morning milk I plucked him off his shelf. It was the first time I had tried to carry him any distance, and his body stiffened, but he allowed me to take him into the barn and put him on the nest. Then he shot out and ran. The next morning I took him in again, and again he bolted. That evening I brought his dinner out to the barn, carried him in, and put him down in front of the plate. He sniffed at it and fled.

Finally I realized what I should have known from the very beginning, that I was going about getting him used to the barn in the wrong way. I brought his dinner in, put it on the floor, went out to make sure he was nearby, then walked in again, and sat down near the plate. After a moment's hesitation he came in to sit beside me, put the two front paws on my lap, and purred so hard that his whole body shook. For a while we stayed like that. Then I picked up the plate to show him the food and put it down again, and while he was busy eating I stole away.

That was how our evening conferences began. After I had taken care of all the chores — in the shortened days of winter that was well after dark — I'd go out with his dinner and a flashlight and find him waiting near the barn, sitting on the snow. He would follow me in and I'd give him the food, but he wouldn't touch it, not until we had had our conference. We'd sit on the floor, and both of us would be shivering with the cold, and I'd explain to him that

I'd have to leave soon, because if I didn't his dinner would freeze. Once, when the temperature was well below zero and a fierce wind was blowing, I turned soft and didn't sit with him, just put the plate down and left, and the next morning I found the food frozen solid, untouched. After that we always had at least a short conference, I well bundled up in a heavy jacket, cap, and mittens, he snuggled against me with the two paws on my lap.

I hoped he would make a nest for himself in the hay, but always I found him in the morning curled up on the floor, about where we had sat during our conference the night before. Although he had grown a thick coat of fur I worried that he might freeze, or at least his ears might get frostbitten, so after some thought I turned a feed barrel over on its side and filled it with hay, and in the evening sat down in front of it with a hand thrust inside to show him it was safe. He slipped in, rustled around in the hay, stroked his head against my hand, and came out to confer and eat.

When I went out with his milk the next morning he was nowhere to be seen, and he did not appear when I called. For a moment I succumbed to panic, then remembered, and put my hand in the barrel. At the far end it encountered his warm body curled up in a deep bowl he had made in the hay.

"Lazybones," I said, and he woke with a start.

He had finally come to regard the hay barn as his home to the extent of at least spending his nights in it, on colder ones in his barrel. But immediately after he'd drunk his morning milk he left. No matter how many times I persuaded him to follow me back in, and no matter how I pleaded with him, he would not stay there during the day. On gloomy and windy days he retired to his disintegrating nest in the old barn, emerging as usual whenever he heard me outside and hastily returning when I went indoors. On bright days he searched out a sunny spot and sat crouched on the snow. I put down a burlap bag and he accepted it gratefully, but his spending hours in the open like that distressed me, so I emptied another feed barrel, dragged it outside, tipped it over just in front of the barn, and filled it with hay. For several days it was ignored. Then one morning he slipped out of it to yawn and stretch and greet me with one of his silent mews, and I had an idea he was particularly pleased with this new accommodation because he was aware of the pleasure it gave me.

There have been various expressions of opinion concerning the ways in which — apart from a peculiar urge to destroy himself and the world — man differs from animals. Until recently it was assumed that man proved his superiority by being able to speak, while animals could not. Now man's conversational capabilities seem to be rapidly diminishing, and we discover that whales and dolphins have quite extensive vocabularies, that apes can carry on fairly complex conversations with humans, even venturing into the abstract. It is said that man is the only animal who takes medicine willingly, that he is the only one who can blush, or, it may be added, needs to. Beyond this we might note that man is the only animal incapable of being completely happy for any length of time. No matter how much he has or is given, he is not satisfied. He has to have more. No matter how far he has traveled, he wants to go farther. Whatever is unobtainable or unattainable becomes something he has to have. In contrast, animals are content with sufficient food to eat and a not-too-uncomfortable place to sleep. They accept without protest the minimum for survival. Anything beyond that is gratefully received, but not expected or demanded.

Asking for nothing, Squeak had attained the nearly unattainable: a rare combination of security and freedom. Although he showed little inclination to wander, even in search of a receptive female, he was free to go wherever he pleased, whenever he pleased. At the same time, he had the security of a home in the barn and a snug retreat in the hay-filled barrel just outside the barn. He could depend on getting his breakfast in the morning and his dinner in the evening. But perhaps most important of all, he had the assurance of my friendship.

Then came the terrible crisis with the goat, and how he endured that period I don't know. We took no more walks in the woods together. There were no more conferences. He was fed, and that was about all. Whether he ate or not I didn't notice. Indeed, for a while I was hardly aware of his existence.

*U*NTIL I STARTED spending summer vacations in the Catskills, some twenty years before the advent of Squeak, I had never even seen a goat except in pictures. About half a mile from the cabin in which I lived on a then sparsely settled road, an old logger named Julian had taken up residence, and he had a goat tethered in his front yard. Her name was Nanny, and she really wasn't much of a goat — potbellied, swaybacked, with only one misshapen horn — but when I said hello she responded so graciously, with close to regal dignity, that I was completely won over. Shrewdly taking note of my enchantment, Julian promptly offered to sell her to me cheap, but I had sense enough to resist. With considerable, occasionally almost insurmountable, difficulties I had managed to transport satchels full of cats to the mountains in the spring and back to New

York in the fall, but making such a trip with a goat, to say nothing of living with one in an apartment, was of course out of the question.

However, Bert, my nearest neighbor barely within shouting distance, had also witnessed my weakness, and perhaps just to tease me took me for a ride one day, slowing down ostentatiously as we came to a field in which two goats were grazing. They were gleaming white and utterly beautiful, a dainty little doe and a buck almost as big as a pony. I may have murmured something or Bert may have just read my mind. Anyway, he backed up and stopped the car and we got out, and that was how I became a permanent resident of the Catskills, and why an abandoned barn stands in back of the house. Although I had previously used a hammer for little more than hanging pictures on walls, I actually built the structure all by myself, even conquering acrophobia to put up the roof, and although it was far from attractive, even, you might say, an eyesore, it stood sturdily against many a high wind and under deep snows through winter after winter.

Fortunately the original plan allowed for expansion, because soon the pair of goats had company. As I had always been given to taking in homeless cats, I now started taking homeless goats, until I had a fair-sized herd, and some of the village children who found it impossible to remember or pronounce my name began to call me Goat Lady. For several years that remained my appellation. Then I worked in the library for a while and was hailed as Lie Berry, which lasted until one of the more literary youngsters read a story of mine and renamed me Writer, which was soon corrupted to Rider, and finally, inexplicably, to Red Rider. Being totally inappropriate, that had quite a short life and I was once again called the Goat Lady, which I accepted with relief because at least it didn't have to be explained to grown-ups.

As Goat Lady I milked and made cheese, and both the milk and the cheese were in such demand that while pleasurably occupied with the milking, and sometimes before drifting off to sleep at night, I dreamed of becoming a real, full-fledged goat farmer. But the perversity of nature brought that to an end.

Because humans favor male puppies and kittens over female, nature prefers that litters of puppies and kittens should contain more females than males. With goats it's the other way around. Because does can be kept and bucks must be got rid of, and there's no way to get rid of a buck unless one has beating in one's breast a stone instead of a heart, nature takes delight in seeing to it that there are more bucks than does. The meat of the young ones is much sought after, especially at Easter time, which has always struck me as being ironic. But there's nothing more entrancing than a prancing kid, nor anything more poignant than its firm belief in the goodness of life. How could one put such trust in the hands of a butcher?

I went begging, sometimes traveling considerable distances, to find what I hoped would be suitable homes for the young bucks, and the end was always the same. Sooner or later, mostly sooner, they would be on someone's dinner table. So when the ingestion of a plastic bag brought about the untimely death of Sam, the sire of the herd, I decided not to replace him and leave goat farming to those with less tendency to become emotionally involved. However, one of the does had already conceived, and in time she produced two kids, a strapping buck I named Samson, and a doe for whom the village children chose the name Pixie, which I hadn't the heart to reject.

They were inseparable, these final offspring of Sam. They slept together, ate together, played together, shrieked if even momentarily parted. Thus I was once again confronted with the same old problem. Separating them, taking Samson away when I knew almost certainly what his fate would be, was something I could not consider. Yet when he came of age there would be more kids born, and more unwanted bucks to dispose of.

That was when an act of fate, cruel in itself, turned out to be for the goats a kindly intervention. Periodically, whenever a peak of population was reached, there would be an outbreak of leptospirosis among the smaller wild animals in the woods. For most of them it was fatal. But transmitted to the goats by infected raccoons, the disease had no effect at all except to make them sterile. So no more young ones were born, and gradually the older does died off, until finally only Pixie and Samson were left.

During the winter they were quartered in the new barn and had to confine their activities to the small exercise yard around it. But in spring, as soon as the grass had grown tall enough, they were let out of the yard to make the trip down the hill to the pasture, and on this momentous day they went quite wild, kicking up their heels and cavorting like kids let out of school.

A small lean-to in the middle of the pasture gave them shelter at night and during rainstorms. On warm days they liked to lie near the fence, in the shade of the big maple trees. Whenever it was cool, they would sit on the big flat rock, forelegs neatly tucked in, to bake in the sun. They had grass and weeds to graze on, and twice a day I gave them grain and water. So it was a good life for them, almost perfect, except for the menace of the dogs.

Tramping along the boundaries of 43,500 square feet of land on a steaming hot summer's day was hardly a pleasant chore, but I walked the pasture fence, around and around, day after day, looking for weak spots and mending them. Yet the dogs still managed to squeeze through, or crawl under, or jump over. While Pixie cowered in their shelter Samson would go out to confront them, holding them at bay, wheeling about to protect his vulnerable flanks, until I heard the barking and ran shouting down the hill to drive the dogs off. I became so alert to such ominous sounds that they would jerk me out of deep sleep even when the sun had not yet lifted from the horizon. But one morning I failed to awaken.

When at the usual hour I took down their grain and water, neither of the goats came to meet me. Pixie was standing as if turned to stone just in front of the shelter. Samson was nowhere to be seen, until a patch of white fur lifted by a gust of wind caught my eye. He was lying in the middle of the pasture, his belly torn, his head gashed, his right foreleg badly chewed. I tried to pull him to his feet and he tried hard to get up, but sank back with a groan.

The day was cold and windy. The sky was heavy with clouds that threatened rain. I ran up the hill to get a blanket and down again to cover him, then went to beg a neighbor for help, and from him I learned what had happened. Just at dawn he had heard dogs barking wildly, had decided to investigate, and had traced the sound to the pasture, where a huge Doberman and a Malemute were leaping and tearing at Samson, one in front, one in back, while he kept turning, trying to fight off one, then the other. He was losing the battle, but when the dogs were driven away he was still standing, and the neighbor thought he had not been badly injured. Now we had somehow to get his two hundred and sixty pounds out of the pasture, where rain was beginning to fall, up the hill, and into the barn, an impossibility for two people, we soon discovered. After a few futile attempts the neighbor went to enlist the help of another man, and with the two of them using the blanket as a sling to half carry, half drag the body while I supported the head, Samson was finally transported to safety.

For three days he lay helpless in his stall. I feared the chewed leg might have been broken, but after some desperate struggling he was back on his feet the fourth day, and a few days later he was hobbling around. Nevertheless, it was weeks before he and Pixie could make the trip back to the pasture, and then they couldn't stay there overnight any more. It was too dangerous.

They slept in the barn, or outside in the yard on warmer nights, and in the morning I opened the gate and led them down the hill. That is, the first few mornings I led them down. From then on they led and I followed, to close the gate after they had entered the pasture. Goats are like that. Any act repeated a few times becomes a habit, a rule that must be adhered to even though the act itself might not be agreeable.

Back in the days when there were a number of goats, one of the older ones had been tied to a fence post each day at five o'clock, for some reason I don't remember although it probably had something to do with the milking routine. One afternoon I heard her screaming as if she were surely being murdered, but when I ran to her rescue I found nothing wrong, except that five o'clock had come and gone and I had neglected to tie her. She had hated being tied, but couldn't bear not to be. A rule was a rule.

So in accordance with this newly established rule Pixie and Samson took themselves down to the pasture, somewhat erratically, straying off course one way or another to play follow the leader, with Pixie always in the lead. Whichever way she went Samson followed precisely. If she hopped over a rock, he in turn hopped over the rock. If she stopped to sniff at something, he stopped and sniffed. She entered the pasture first, he was right behind her, and right behind him I came along to close the gate.

That's the way it was in the morning. In the evening the order was reversed. I'd stand at the gate and call, "You want to go home?" and somewhere in the pasture two white forms would rise and amble lazily toward me, with Samson in the lead. When I opened the gate there was no dawdling or cavorting. The return home was a strictly no-nonsense trip. Solemnly Samson marched up the hill with Pixie at his heels, and I had to take care not to be in their way, because if they encountered me on the path they simply shoved me off. Staying on the path for their return to the barn was, it seemed, another hard-and-fast rule.

I had a rule of my own, never to go home empty-handed. After the trip to the pasture on nice mornings I'd spend perhaps half an hour gathering and piling firewood up near the gate, and each evening I'd select a piece to carry back with me. Once when I started up the path and heard the goats coming behind me I quickly sidestepped to get out of the way as usual, but the log I'd chosen was a long one that jutted over the path. Only a couple of steps would have taken them around it, but to remain on the path and thus adhere to the rule, first Samson ducked under the log, then Pixie ducked.

Another strict, absolutely inviolable rule was one that Samson enforced. I was not allowed to touch Pixie.

Many bucks tend to be unpredictably ill-tempered, especially during mating season, which lasts from late fall until early spring, and association with them at this time can be hazardous. But Samson was always a perfect gentleman. True, he loved to tease, snatching things out of my pockets and dashing off, daring me to try to get them back, or yanking buttons off my jacket or grazing in my hair, occasionally actually removing a mouthful, and whenever I stooped over he positively could not resist sampling the soft part of my anatomy thus made prominent. But he never seriously threatened me unless I violated this one rule of his, and even then he refrained from bucking, perhaps because he considered such behavior beneath his dignity. Instead he would just fling himself against me, and being sideswiped by his powerful body was rather like getting hit by a truck. Unless I managed to grab something to hold on to I'd go sprawling.

I never could figure out whether he wouldn't let me touch Pixie because he was jealous and resented any attention paid to her, or whether he was overly protective of her. Giving in to this whim of his was easy enough most of the time, but every so often Pixie's hooves had to be trimmed. To keep her from flouncing around during this operation I had to enlist the help of a neighbor, and of course two people handling her was twice as bad as only one.

One time we outwitted Samson by letting him out of the pasture toward the end of the day, then closing the gate so Pixie couldn't follow. He trotted up the path a little way, suddenly realized she was not behind him as usual, turned and came tearing down, tried to bulldoze his way back into the pasture and, when he didn't succeed, paced to and fro in front of the gate like an expectant father awaiting the arrival of his firstborn, all the while letting out nerve-shattering howls.

Next time, we tried the opposite, letting out Pixie, who was always the first to leave the yard in the morning, and slamming the gate shut to imprison Samson. That turned out to be, if anything, even worse. Backing off a little way to get good momentum, he charged time after time, ramming his head against the gate like a wrecking ball, almost tearing it off the heavy hinges. And this time his deafening bellows were augmented by unearthly wails from Pixie, emitted perhaps in sympathy, perhaps only in protest, because she hated having her hooves trimmed.

As they grew older their strong attachment to each other made me increasingly uneasy. Barring some fortuitous accident, such as their being struck simultaneously by a lethal bolt of lightning, they were one day bound to be separated. Which would be the first to go? And how would it be for the one that was left? Time had slowed them down a bit. They left the yard in the morning somewhat less exuberantly, made the trip down the hill more sedately, but neither showed any signs of real physical decline. They were well fleshed out, their muscles were firm, their coats gleaming, their eyes bright, their teeth still strong and sharp, as was proved to me well enough if I left a finger in the way while offering peanuts — they would do anything to get a reward of peanuts.

When they were fifteen the placid routine of their lives was a trifle disrupted by my persuading Squeak to reside in the other half of their barn. Since they would have made a mess out of the hay stored in that half, they were never allowed in it, so they did not actually meet Squeak, may not have known exactly who the new arrival was. They were aware, however, of a presence where one had not been before, but remained indifferent to it as long as they believed me to be doing likewise. What they simply could not stand was hearing me converse with this unknown during our evening conferences. I tried whispering to Squeak instead of speaking out loud, then not speaking at all, but they still knew I was there with him, not with them. To attract my attention they shuffled around, emitting heartrending moans, clattered over the floor, pacing back and forth, rubbed their bodies against the intervening wall, and finally Samson fell back on his bulldozer tactics, ramming his head against the wall in an effort to break it down.

Squeak went on purring, evidently not at all bothered by the racket, but when thuds shook the entire barn I gave in, said good night to him and went around to the goats' entrance, to hand out a few conciliatory peanuts and confer with them for a while. Thus a new routine was established, and as was their custom they adapted to it, waiting patiently while I conferred with Squeak, having faith in my adherence to the rule that promised they'd be next.

Although there was absolutely no reason for it,

toward winter's end my concern over their welfare increased. I kept careful watch, made sure they ate all of their grain, checked for the slightest signs of disability, sometimes even went out in the middle of the night to make sure that they were safe. There was never anything wrong, yet apprehension mounted. And finally, with no warning, there was justification.

Early one morning I was awakened by the barking of dogs. That was not unusual. Practically every household for miles around had at least one dog, and each dog seemed determined to outdo a rooster in proclaiming that the sun was rising. I had grown used to being startled out of sleep at dawn, not infrequently had hopped out of bed and rushed outside, only to discover that the barking was well down the road and merely seemed close in the thin morning air. But this time it really was close. It was just in back of the house. It was in the goat yard.

Without even stopping to put on shoes I ran outside. There were two dogs, Malemutes, as big as wolves. Samson was backed against the far side of the fence, trying to protect his flanks. The dogs were leaping around him, dodging his vainly slashing forefeet, one darting in for a quick snap while he tried to fend off the other. As I fumbled to open the gate I yelled. Samson heard me and responded with a desperate howl. The dogs paid no attention. I looked around for some kind of weapon, a stick or a rock, and remembered the crosscut saw hanging on a hook in the barn. In blind rage I took it and flailed wildly, not knowing or caring how the sharp teeth of the blade cut into flesh, hardly hearing the yelps of pain and fear, coming to my senses only after the dogs had found and plunged out through the break they had made in the fence.

Samson was trembling violently, but seemed unhurt. I led him into the barn, where Pixie was also trembling, and stayed there for a while talking to them and stroking Samson until the wildness went out of his eyes. Then I mended the fence, returned to the house, and got back into bed to stop my own trembling.

I hadn't noticed that the sky was overcast, nor had I been at all aware of the damp chill in the air. But when I woke again at the usual hour I found it a most unpleasant day, windy and cold, with a light rain falling. I filled the goats' bucket with warm water and put their grain in a container — always the first thing I did when I got up — and started toward the barn, then dropped everything when I saw a white mound lying in the middle of the yard.

It was Samson, crying feebly, evidently the victim of a heart attack. I pulled at him, trying to get him back on his feet. He couldn't even lift his head. His eyes full of terror begged for help, but all I could do was put a blanket over him and again call on neighbors for help.

In the barn he lay hour after hour, not moving, only following me with his eyes and answering weakly when I spoke to him. The rain changed to snow and a fierce wind blew from the north. It was a vicious day. I filled plastic bottles with hot water and banked them all around him and covered him with a second blanket, but still he was icy cold. I gave him a swallow of vodka and he stopped crying, closed his eyes, and seemed to sleep. Only his shallow breathing told me he was still alive.

Every hour I changed the bottles, tucking the hot ones under the blankets all around him, and they seemed to give his body some warmth, but his legs remained cold, even when I tried to rub life back into them. When darkness came the cold invaded my body, too. Bundled as I was in a heavy jacket, I still could not stop shivering. Around midnight I realized that was probably because I had had no dinner, so I made some tea and ate a few crackers. Then I was out with Samson again and found him awake, trying to talk to me, his voice hardly audible. I lay on top of the blankets with an arm around his neck to warm and comfort him, and for a while he was quiet. Then just as the first light came into the sky he breathed deeply, once, again, and again, and then he was not breathing any more.

*T*HE WIND DIED down and the sun came out and the snow melted. It turned into a lovely day. Samson looked so well that it seemed he must surely come to life and rise and walk again, and so peaceful that I couldn't bear to disturb him. All of that day he lay in his stall with the blankets covering him, and Pixie took no notice. She ate her grain, munched on hay, placidly chewed her cud as usual. Perhaps she thought he was only sleeping.

In the evening I gave Squeak his dinner and sat with him briefly in a conference that was the last we'd have in a long time, then went around to enter the unaccustomed hush in the other side of the barn. Pixie was lying with her neck curved like a swan's to rest her head on her shoulder. She woke slowly, almost reluctantly, accepted a few peanuts as if she were conferring a favor on me, and didn't beg for more. I said good night to her, then, with the feeling that he was still there and able to hear, said good night to Samson, too.

The next day a man came to help me bury Samson. His body was even heavier in death than in life, and we had to drag him out of the barn. "The terrible indignity of dying," I said, and the man gave me a puzzled look. Then we heard an anguished wail. Pixie was just behind us, trying to get to Samson. I took her back into the barn and shut her up so she couldn't watch us putting him into his grave, but she kept on crying. Hour after hour she cried, all through the rest of the day and all through the night. It was so un-nerving that Squeak didn't come to eat his dinner, and when I checked several times during the night he was not in his nest.

As soon as morning came I opened the gate and let Pixie out of the yard, thinking that being allowed to roam might distract her, but it only made her worse. In wild desperation she ran around the house, down and up the path to the pasture, through the yard, into and out of the barn, searching for Samson, calling to him, screaming for him. It was agonizing to watch and listen to, and it went on for all of that day, and the next, and the next.

At sundown Squeak appeared, but could not be persuaded to go anywhere near the barn. At a safe distance he sat gazing at his home, until finally I put his dinner on the shelf outside the kitchen window, just as in the old days, and lifted him onto it so he could eat. Where he went after that I didn't notice, nor did I know where he spent the night. Possibly he went back to his old nest in the abandoned barn.

Then on the fourth day Pixie suddenly became quiet, too quiet. She refused to leave the barn. I put a rope around her neck and led her outside to her dish of grain but she would not eat, and the moment she was set free she went back into the barn. Ignoring the fresh hay I had put in her stall she went into Samson's, where his scent no doubt lingered, and, settling down on his bed, turned her gaze inward, refusing even to acknowledge my presence.

The next day the water in her bucket was still at the same level and her grain had not been touched. I carried out fresh warm water and put the bucket directly in front of her, but she stared past it as if it didn't exist. The day after that she still hadn't moved, and I knew she was growing weak. I pulled her up and made her stand. She sank to her knees. I forced her to get up again and held her up and made her walk a few steps, rewarding her with bits of apple that I almost had to shove into her mouth.

The day after that she drank some water, and lured by bits of apple she took a few feeble steps after me. Then each day I managed to lead her a little farther away from Samson's bed, outside the barn, through the gate, and finally to the field in front of the house. Once she started grazing there she seemed to forget all about me, yet even though her back was turned and I made no sound, she started crying the moment I left. I had to go back and stay with her again, and that's how it was from then on. Every day I took her to the field and stayed with her to persuade her to eat.

Goats have long memories. I don't think they ever really forget anything. Once when there were too many goats to care for properly I gave one away. Two years later her new owner died, and I took her back. When the truck that brought her was still on the road she started bleating with excitement, and as soon as she was free she ran straight into the barn, with little cries of joy. After a long, long exile, she was *home* again.

I was sure that Pixie hadn't forgotten Samson, but at least she seemed to have accepted and adjusted to his absence. Then one day when we went to the field she kept on going, following the path down the hill all the way to the pasture, and just inside the gate she stood quite still, only turning her head to look this way and that. It was as if she had made up her mind that she would will Samson into being, that she would find him there, where they had spent so many years together. For a long time she didn't move. Then she turned slowly and came back up the hill.

After that she did no more searching. Poor substitute though I was, I took Samson's place as her companion. Wherever I went out of doors she was with me, trotting back and forth and around while I took care of various chores, in what must have seemed to her like utterly senseless meandering. If I stayed any length of time in a spot that offered something to eat, she grazed. Otherwise she simply stood and waited for me to go elsewhere. If a car turned into the driveway she had to go with me to see who was in it, and if a visitor engaged in conversation with me she stood gravely at my side, reminding me of a youngster hanging about listening to grown-ups talk, turning her head to gaze at one or the other of us as we spoke, as though understanding every word. Like a white shadow she stayed with me until I went indoors. Then she simply sat near the house and waited for me to come out again.

During most of this period Squeak remained in attendance, but at a distance. When we went to the field each day he also went to the field, but not really with us, only going in the same direction, and as long as we were there he was there, a remote figure sitting on a rock, gazing intently at me, glancing quickly away to check on Pixie's movements and staring at me again, until I spoke to him. Then he was at once withdrawn, lost in thought, unaware of my existence. There seemed to be no way I could win him back, until one day when the ground was wet after an early morning rain I took a burlap bag to sit on.

Where the field gave way to a dense growth of maple saplings there was a rock almost as flat and smooth as the one in the pasture. As I spread the burlap bag on it I saw out of the corner of my eye that he was watching, and as soon as I sat down on the bag he came running over to fling himself down beside me. "Welcome back," I said, and abandoning customary dignity he rolled over to offer his belly in total surrender.

Every morning after that he was sitting near the barn waiting for us, and the three of us would form a strange procession, sometimes with him in the lead, sometimes me, sometimes Pixie. When the field was finally grazed over so that little was left for Pixie to eat we went elsewhere, ranging in all directions. While Pixie sampled the leaves of various bushes and saplings, I gathered firewood, and Squeak snuffled around to read in the earth stories about the passage of other animals.

The woodlot on the other side of the brook was where I could find the best firewood, and also where Squeak liked best to go, but Pixie refused to accompany us there. She was afraid of the water. Squeak could leap from one stepping stone to another so lightly that he almost seemed to float through the air, and I traversed safely enough, though with less agility, but no amount of coaxing could persuade Pixie to try the stones, even when the water was shallow and swirled around them with scarcely a ripple.

Finally I went on a hunt for flat rocks, and while she poked around, nibbling at this and that, and Squeak sat watching, I built a bridge, putting down one layer of rocks with spaces between for the water to flow through, and another layer on top to provide solid footing. I walked over and over it, adjusting one rock or the other to make sure there would be not the slightest joggling, then went to the other side and called. Pixie put two feet on the first rock, snorted, backed off and wailed. She didn't trust my bridge.

I returned to her, got behind her, and pushed. Her rear went up in the air, her forefeet remained firmly planted. So I led the procession back to the barn to put a rope around her neck, and the three of us started out once more. Again she balked when we got to the bridge. Standing in the middle of it I braced myself and gave a mighty heave on the rope, and all of a sudden, in a wild plunge that almost knocked me into the water, she clattered over.

On the other side she needed no more coaxing. This was for her virgin territory, full of all kinds of good things to eat, sugar maples and young birch trees and Quaker lady wherever there was a clearing. She munched happily, I picked up firewood, and Squeak searched out a place where there was sunlight to bask in sleepy-eyed, until I stopped working and sat down. Then he joined me, and it was like listening to a symphony, the throb of his purring, the rustling of leaves as Pixie moved among them, the murmuring of the brook, the chattering of an invisible squirrel, the percussion of a woodpecker tapping on a tree somewhere overhead, and everywhere outside our concert hall complete silence, not even marred by the distant barking of a dog.

"We could be far back in the woods, far back in time," I said to Squeak. "Back in the days when there were no roads, no cars, no houses, no people, only miles and miles of wilderness on all sides."

How long would we last in such an environment? We, all three of us, were products of civilization, needing those roads and cars and houses and people for survival. Yet thoughts of returning to the primitive were enticing, offering the security of being completely controlled by nature, eliminating the need ever to make a decision. Then the far-off shouting of children broke the spell, and our wilderness returned to being only a small woodlot in a bustling world.

The next day Squeak and I started toward the brook, and Pixie came along willingly enough until we reached the bridge. I pleaded and she put her forefeet on it gingerly and backed away.

"You're on your own," I told her. "Don't be such a coward."

Squeak and I walked on toward the woods. In desolate wails she beseeched us to come back. We kept on going. When we were out of sight among the trees the wails rose to piercing shrieks, and stopped abruptly.

"Maybe we'd better go back," I said to Squeak. Then we heard footsteps, and there was Pixie on our side of the bridge, triumphantly catching up with us.

She never did get over her fear of the brook, and summoning up courage to make the crossing always took a while. She would try the first rock, change her mind, start eating some weed as if it were a particularly choice morsel, eye the bridge, approach it to try the first rock again, and suddenly make such a wild dash over that I had to get out of the way fast, or she'd probably have tossed me into the air. But once this crisis was past she found our excursions most satisfactory.

Each day we went the same way. Each day was almost exactly like the one before, uneventful but full of quiet enjoyment, until something else came along to distract me and once again try Squeak's patience.

B ACK IN THE TIME when Squeak and I were not so well acquainted, one of my chores each day was to make a quick trip to the woods to, I hoped, get rid of Pest. The explanation for this goes still further back, to the days when I was known as Lie Berry and was credited with extraordinary powers barely falling short of being able to resurrect the dead. The fact that I so often failed even to heal the sick made no difference. With undiminished faith, youngsters brought to me injured birds, wounded squirrels, ailing kittens, and on one memorable occasion buckets and buckets of frogs, rescued from a pond about to be drained. Actually the frogs weren't too much of a problem. They were simply sloshed out of bucket after bucket into the brook, where they dispersed in all directions.

Nor did it seem to involve too much trouble when

one day a little girl came to me with tears running down her cheeks and a small box clutched in her hands. Having run an errand or done a favor — that part of her story, being unimportant, was vague — she had earned a small sum of money, and where should money be spent but in a pet shop? Fortunately, or perhaps unfortunately, most of the animals for sale were beyond her means, but she did have sufficient funds to purchase two white mice. They were in a box that she held out to me, with tears running down her cheeks. Her mother had taken one look at them and said, "Out!"

The little girl knew perfectly well that I had a large outdoor cage, a ten-foot walk-in, which had originally housed squirrels but was then vacant, and she also knew perfectly well what my reaction to her sad story would be. Yes, of course she could put the mice in the cage. What harm was there in giving sanctuary to a couple of homeless mice?

I soon found out. The mice, so beautiful, like dainty jewels with their little pink eyes set in gleaming white fur, turned out to be a pair. In no time at all there were were twelve, then twenty-five, a hundred — a thousand. The coffee cans in which they lived, lined up several layers deep along one side of the cage, resembled a large housing project, and since the mice proved to be atrocious housekeepers, I spent hours tidying up for them, removing old bedding and putting in fresh. No matter which can I chose, it invariably contained a mound of squirming, naked, wormlike babies to further augment the population, with several mothers, or what I presumed to be mothers, lying on top of the heap. My invasion always provoked a wild exodus, the grown-ups seizing babies in their mouths and scurrying off to deposit them in a neighboring can, where presumably other mothers with heaps of babies did not object to sharing quarters. I'd scoop up the remaining progeny and carefully put them to one side, and while I housecleaned, the mothers would return again and again, to pick up more babies and carry them off, until none was left. Whether they brought them all back to enjoy the clean bedding I didn't know, but when I got to the end of the row and started at the beginning again, it seemed to me I always found the same heap of babies guarded over by the same mothers.

The little girl responsible for this population explosion paid a visit every once in a while to watch while I did the housecleaning and to gaze with awe at the swarm that gathered around the communal tray at feeding time. "It's creepy," she'd say with a delicate shudder, and not a trace of remorse.

It was not only creepy. It was expensive.

I put enormous quantities of food in the cage — sunflower seeds, corn, cereal, popcorn, peanuts, apples, cat chow, raisins, bread. It vanished. Operating on the theory that if nothing was left over there hadn't been enough, I increased the amounts and still everything was gone. I found it hard to believe that even an army of mice, the equivalent of which I was indeed harboring, could consume so much so quickly, and I finally found out it actually didn't. Making an unscheduled visit to the cage one morning I heard a trill of alarm and caught a glimpse of something, I didn't know exactly what, whisking out of sight behind the housing complex. Precipitating a near-riot of mice tumbling out of all the doorways, I moved some of the houses and found the solution to where whoever the invader was had gone. A neat little tunnel had been dug to gain entrance to the cage. Somebody from outside was slipping through the tunnel to steal the mouse food.

That night I baited a Haveaheart trap with five peanuts and placed it with the entrance close enough against the tunnel so that none of the resident mice could get it. The next morning I found imprisoned a somewhat frightened, thoroughly outraged chipmunk. It opened its mouth to squawk at the sight of me, and out spewed ten peanut kernels, plus some small seeds that must have been picked up elsewhere.

With the trap dancing erratically as the chipmunk scurried around in it trying to find a way out, I took a walk in the woods and searched until I found a rocky ledge that looked like a suitable shelter. When the door of the trap was opened, out shot the chipmunk to disappear at once under the ledge. I gave back the ten peanut kernels it had lost, added a few extra nuts to provide a good start in this new location, said good-bye and good riddance, and went back home to shove a stone into the tunnel that had been dug to gain entrance to the mouse cage.

The next morning I found I had underestimated the determination and also the strength of a chipmunk. The stone had been removed from the tunnel, and again the mouse food had been stolen. I set the trap a second time and again caught the thief, as outraged as before but not quite so frightened. Again I took him to the woods and left a supply of nuts for him, and on the way back found a fairly heavy boulder to shove against the tunnel.

The following morning there was a new tunnel dug next to the big boulder that was plugging the old one.

Thus began a daily routine with Pest. Old tunnels were plugged, new tunnels were dug. Each morning I went for a walk, and Pest got so used to being carried to the woods that he no longer made the trap dance with his efforts to get out. He just sat quietly taking in the sights as if rather enjoying the trip, and he got to know the way back home so well that his return coincided with mine. Then, being fleeter of foot, he actually began arriving ahead of me, so he could have the diversion of watching me stop up his latest tunnel.

And finally, to make it quite clear that he had no intention of giving up such a good location, he spent afternoons bounding into the woods and out again, to carry back the nuts I had left to persuade him to reside elsewhere.

There seemed to be no way short of murder to get rid of him, and I was ready to concede defeat, when his tactics changed. Either he came to the conclusion that after we had taken so many trips together we must be friends, or else he just got tired of digging tunnels, especially since finding places for new ones between boulders was growing increasingly difficult. Anyway, instead of doing all that work he took to begging, which, as is often the case, turned out to be much more profitable.

This required me to keep nuts readily available at all times, because from the moment I first appeared outside in the morning until the end of the day, there was Pest at my feet, demanding tribute. Taking care as a rule not to grab my finger instead of a nut, he'd accept my offering, try it for size in one cheek pouch, shift it to the one on the other side and maneuver it around until it caused not too much discomfort, beg for another nut to put in the first pouch, chew it into place, and ask for a third nut to carry between his teeth. Rattling like a castanet he'd scamper off to deposit this treasure in his bank vault and return almost immediately for another handout, or, if I happened to be sitting or kneeling, save me trouble by plunging into a pocket to help himself.

Soon he was also making it easier for me when I was standing by shinnying up my pants leg as far as a pocket. If I happened to be preoccupied this was somewhat disconcerting, as it most certainly was whenever someone came calling. While the visitor and I stood talking, Pest would suddenly appear to scramble up a leg, and the trouble was that for him a leg was a leg, never mind to whom it was attached. The startled visitor had to be reassured — the leg scaler was only a chipmunk, and quite healthy, not mad — then hastily handed some nuts to extricate Pest from a pocket, or persuade him to stop scurrying around at hip level in search of one.

Most people wore slacks, which Pest could scale without difficulty, but one day a very fat woman wearing a dress stopped by. We stood talking for a few moments, then all at once she began hopping about in a wild Indian war dance that had me transfixed with awe, certain that I was witnessing some terrible seizure, until the cause of her contortions appeared at the neckline. A leg being a leg with or without pants, Pest had climbed one of hers, ducked under the dress, traveled around and around the vast interior, perhaps in search of a pocket, and finally emerged at, so to speak, the summit. Fortunately the woman was as good-natured as fat people are supposed to be, and Pest made a safe though precipitous descent.

In time even Pixie was subjected to bold advances, and attempts to climb her legs were thwarted only by a vigorous stamping of hooves. However, she did allow him to hop into her feeding dish to share her breakfast, which he did with apparently no fear of getting gobbled up along with a mouthful of grain. While she stood near the dish waiting for me to fill it he would even sit up before her to beg, perhaps in the belief that she herself somehow produced the grain before ingesting it.

He had to work fast to outrace her and get his pouches filled before the dish was empty, then make a long trip to take the load to his home. Never did he eat so much as a kernel in the dish, or stop on the way to sample what he was carrying. In fact, transportation took up so much of his time that I often wondered when he did eat, and also how he managed to get any work done on his house, which I suspected was a veritable mansion.

An occasional chipmunk may be shiftless enough to live like a squatter under a barn or in someone's cellar, but Pest belonged to the respectable majority dwelling in style underground, with one room for sleeping, as many more as might be needed for storage, and, off a little way at a lower level, a bathroom. A lucky chipmunk like Pest, having access to an unlimited supply of nuts, has to keep on adding storage rooms, which involves a great deal of work. Soil must be dug out, shoved up through the tunnel to the surface, then pushed some distance away, so that no mound near the entrance will betray the fact that a recent excavation has been made.

Pest's two entrances, his front and back doors, you might say, were eight feet apart. Sometimes as I watched him popping in and out I tried to imagine what it was like down there where he lived below the frost line. He must have had many rooms and no doubt kept them very tidy, for he gave evidence of being a fussy housekeeper. With nuts crammed into his mouth, one day he rattled around as if he'd quite forgotten where he lived, actually passing right by one of his entrances without seeming to see it. Finally I realized I was the cause of this erratic behavior. Camera in hand to try to get a picture of him, I was kneeling on his back door, and carrying foodstuffs through the front door was apparently unthinkable.

Some animals, and humans also for that matter, seem to be especially favored by fate, and Pest was certainly one of the chosen. In a word full of hazards, with the likelihood of his becoming a delectable mouthful for some predator at practically any moment, he flitted about within a charmed circle of certainty that nothing unpleasant could possibly happen to him, and maybe because he was so certain, nothing did. I worried about an eventual encounter with Squeak, who after all was a cat, uncharacteristically tolerant of birds and squirrels and mice and moths, to be sure, but perhaps less so of anything as arrogant and careless as Pest.

Miraculously, it was some time before they met. Whenever Pest came begging, Squeak's back was turned, or he was dozing in the sun, or drinking his milk, or having his lunch. And whenever someone came to visit, which was when Pest dearly loved to put on a show, Squeak always fled. He was terrified of strangers.

But one day when I was sitting on a rock with Squeak beside me as usual, Pest came bounding over to invade a pocket as usual. He saw Squeak well enough but must have decided this was some strange appendage that had grown out of me since we'd last met, and as such, worthy of inspection. He went straight to Squeak, touched noses, reacted as if given a charge of electricity, and leaped away. Squeak blinked with surprise, watched the hasty retreat with some interest, then just looked bored.

Even in flight Pest must have taken note of this un-catlike behavior, because each day thereafter he became a little bolder, until caution was so completely abandoned that if the shortest distance between where he was and I was had Squeak in the way, his body was simply walked over. Needless to say Squeak found being part of a highway not much to his liking, especially when he was jerked out of a doze, and to spare him annoyance I would keep a lookout and shout, "No, Pest, don't run over Squeak!"

Nevertheless, his patience continued to be tried until a day came when Pest's behavior changed abruptly. Appearing as usual in the morning, he made no attempt to climb my leg but passed me by as if I had ceased to exist in corporeal form. I held out a nut and called to him, and he paid no attention. Nosing around here and there, he seemed to be hunting for something. I threw a nut to him. He stopped to examine it, let it lie, and continued searching, sniffing at one leaf, and another, and another, until he came to one that seemed to interest him. Holding it between his paws he gave it a close inspection, then crumpled and stuffed it into his pouch. After more searching he found another to his liking — both were beech leaves — and with a portion of this second one protruding from his mouth he ran off to his den. And after that we saw no more of him.

For days I expected him to appear at almost any moment. Sometimes I would think I heard him rustling in the leaves and I'd call out his name, and Squeak would look this way and that, evidently also expecting to see him and maybe be used as a highway again. Then he'd relax and sigh, no doubt with relief.

But what had happened to Pest? His sudden lack of interest in nuts and his strange preoccupation with the leaves was puzzling, until I remembered how, a long time ago, I had watched Midge behaving in very much the same way.

BECAUSE STORES are fairly distant, I go shopping only once a week, and fear that I'll run out of something between trips always impels me to buy more than I need. Nature seems to have the same propensity. To ensure adequate supplies she produces excessive quantities of everything from seeds to people, then — with the exception of people, who so far have managed to outwit her — ruthlessly discards the surplus.

I can think of only one instance in which a reduction in population is made humanely, if that term is at all applicable to nature, and this is in the delightful newt–eft relationship. Newts are small greenish brown salamanders that may be seen darting about or resting in the silt at the bottom of ponds or quiescent pools in small streams. They breed normally and produce eggs normally and the eggs hatch normally, but from then on strange things may happen. Instead of becoming newts like their parents, some of the young ones may turn into efts, and the controlling factor seems to be how the population relates to the environment.

If there's plenty of room in the pond, most of the eggs will evolve into aquatic newts and remain in the pond. But if lack of rainfall reduces the size of the pond and it becomes too crowded, most of the young will become land-dwelling efts, beautiful, fragile, bright red little salamanders that live mostly under rocks or moist piles of leaves and seldom venture abroad unless it rains. Then they may be seen, sometimes in great numbers, on country roads and paths and clearings in the woods. However, they may not remain efts. As soon as conditions in the pond improve and there's room for an increase in population, the little efts grow larger, change color, return to the water, and become aquatic newts. What is fascinating about this arrangement is that while efts remain efts, which may be as long as seven years, they are sexually immature. They cannot mate or reproduce until they turn into newts. In other words, you could say that efts are newts kept "on hold," to guarantee the survival of the species while making no contribution to overpopulation.

This neat way of preventing the buildup of a surplus is so gentle and so ingenious that it almost makes one believe that there is some kindness as well as efficiency in nature. But alas, it is the exception. For most other species the reduction of population is capricious and brutal. Breeding is allowed to continue unabated far beyond supportable levels. Then there's a sudden outbreak of disease, usually involving considerable, often prolonged, suffering, that kills by the hundreds. Before one such epidemic I counted thirty-five raccoons visiting our house at night. After nature made the mandatory correction, only two remained. But these two found mates somewhere and the next year each produced four babies, bringing the total up to ten. And with nature once more looking the other way for a while, a high of thirty-five would no doubt be reached again, to be followed by another epidemic.

Instead of disease, starvation may be the means of eliminating smaller animals. There will be an autumn in which trees bear no fruit or nuts, and seeds are "false," with no kernels in them. With nothing to store to tide them over the winter or even keep them alive from day to day, rodents wander about vainly in search of food, or else migrate in the hope of coming upon better conditions elsewhere. In one truly spectacular migration, squirrels on both sides of the Hudson River swam to the other side, those on the west to the east, those on the east to the west, and when it ended, both banks of the river were littered with their bodies.

It was in such a tragic year of famine that I acquired all the chipmunks.

That was back in the days when the house cats were allowed to go out of doors during the day. Not until I began finding dead birds on the floor did I realize how much damage they were doing. The fault was of course not theirs, but mine. We are as we are made. The cats were no more to blame for possessing hunting instincts than I was for having, say, brown eyes instead of blue. I was the one to blame for allowing that instinct to have such free rein. The wild cat, or the feral cat, has so hard a time just surviving that it does little hunting except for food, the male only to feed himself, the female to feed her young also. In the well-fed house cat the instinct remains, but the reason for it has been eliminated. Deeply imbedded in the female is the urge to bring home food for her young, even if she has no young.

In time I became aware of a tendency to specialize. Scorpio brought home only snakes, dragging them with some difficulty between her legs. Except for some superficial nicks around their middles they were usually unharmed, and once her obligation was discharged she had no objection to their being returned to the wild. Kate was partial to catching frogs, but since most felines find the taste of frogs somewhat disagreeable, and she was no exception, they suffered little or no damage. Cricket adjusted to civilization by spending the better part of her days traveling to and fro, transporting bones from a boarding house which evidently served a lot of chicken and either gave her handouts or was careless in disposing of garbage. You could say the bones were unharmed, too, because nobody showed the slightest interest in them after they were delivered. Sera — whose full name was, ironically, Seraphim — had a most regrettable weakness for birds, and it was this proclivity of hers that eventually led to everyone's incarceration.

In that year of famine, however, they all gave up their specialties to concentrate on mice and chipmunks, because there were so many wandering around, and in their weakened state they were so easy to catch.

The mice that were brought home were taken to the barn, where I hoped they would find enough seeds in the hay to sustain them until better times, but I hadn't the heart to turn out the emaciated chipmunks. I made a roomy cage for Napper, the first to arrive, and to approximate normal living conditions gave him two boxes, one for sleeping, one for storing foodstuffs. What I didn't know then was that chipmunks simply can't abide each other. Put two together and you're likely to have only one in a few days, or even a few hours. When another cat presented me with Bricks — so named because she was housed briefly in a cardboard box bearing the enigmatic legend, No. 469 bricks — I simply put her in with Napper, and just to disprove an absolutely unbreakable rule they got along beautifully, sharing bed and board without a trace of animosity except for the first time I robbed them.

Probably no creature on earth is more addicted to hoarding than a chipmunk. Napper and Bricks spent most of their waking hours begging for nuts that were at once taken to the storehouse and tamped in vigorously to make sure of a tight fit. But space was limited, and in spite of such care, nuts started cascading out of the doorway and had to be constantly shoved back in. Nevertheless, the chipmunks continued to beg and crammed the overflow into their sleeping box, then rattled around during the night on a bed so bumpy that sleeping was difficult.

One morning Napper evidently decided that living conditions had become intolerable and some of the nuts would have to go. Their feeding tray was taken out and cleaned each day, and having become accustomed to this service they always placed on it whatever they wished to throw away. Now, along with apple peels, empty nut shells, and scraps of paper, the bothersome nuts were put on the tray, lined up all around the edges, carefully sorted as to size and kind. Both chipmunks then spent some time rearranging their bedding, adding the fresh tissues I had given them, and after that Napper went around and around the tray examining all the discarded nuts, touching them, poking back one or the other that had rolled slightly out of line, and finally he made up his mind. All the bedding was taken out of the house, all the nuts were carried back in, the bedding was thrown on top of them, and the chipmunks suffered through another uncomfortable night.

So I robbed them. When I was fairly certain they were sound asleep I stealthily removed their storehouse, emptied out the nuts, and slipped it back in again. But, unfortunately, Bricks either heard me or else was awakened by an untimely hunger. She got out of bed, went to the storehouse, stood in the doorway for a moment, then let out a shriek. Hurrying back to Napper she woke him, and together they went to inspect the empty storehouse. For a while they just pattered around inside. Then they began arguing, perhaps each accusing the other of having stolen the nuts. Their voices grew louder and louder, and finally they were screaming at each other and rolling around in such a brawl that I had to put a hand in to stop them.

The next day they were once more friends, but suspicious of each other. Whenever one went into the storehouse the other followed, no doubt to make sure there would be no more filching. But chipmunks are quick to learn and readily adaptable. Although they may never have comprehended the reason for my occasional night raids, they came to accept them. What they found absolutely unacceptable was my introducing Pete.

There used to be a woman down the road who vacuumed, dusted, scrubbed, and polished her floors every day, and all visitors as well as members of her family had to remove their shoes before entering her immaculate domain. Bricks and Napper reminded me of her. Everything in their cage had to be spotless. Every few days their old bedding was piled on the tray for removal, and fresh tissue was carried in to be spread and carefully tamped down. Only one corner of the tray, always the same corner, was used for sanitary purposes. Nuts in the storehouse were inspected to make sure they were in good condition. Sometimes one that I thought looked perfectly all right was singled out and put on the tray, and if offered again was rejected. Invariably I would discover the kernel inside the shell had started to go bad, or had shriveled. Perishables were not kept from one day to the next but were put on the tray and covered with shredded paper.

All this meticulous housekeeping was undone when a cat brought in Pete and, still not aware of a chipmunk's unsocial tendencies, I put him in the cage with the other two, with, however, a separate box to sleep in.

Undoubtedly a member of the squatter class, Pete

was a downright slob. He dirtied the water dish, crammed perishables into the storehouse, even took berries and pieces of banana and apples to bed with him. Bricks and Napper were constantly having to clean up after the messes he made. No doubt that contributed to their growing animosity, but most likely he wouldn't have been tolerated anyway. At first there was only some fairly strenuous bickering, but soon they began beating him up so severely that I finally had to remove him to save his life.

In the second cage I built he lived in solitary, slovenly contentment until I was given Becky. She lost no time in protesting against being quartered with Pete, and again he was beaten up. So I made a third cage to house her, then a fourth cage for Nix, so named because she didn't seem to like anybody or anything, including, I suspected, herself. A fifth cage was made to accommodate still another arrival, solemn, dignified Mr. Perkins; a sixth for Gramps, an old fellow who wanted only to finish out his life in peace; and a seventh for Midge, a happy-go-lucky little show-off who loved to turn somersaults for the amusement of — and handouts from — visitors.

Since floor space was limited, the cages were piled one on top of the other, like so many units in an apartment house, which gave each occupant the diversion of feuding with a neighbor. Gramps lost half his tail when he absentmindedly let it dangle through the wire into the cage below, and most of the others ended up minus a toe or two because they couldn't resist taunting whoever lived above by scampering upside down across their ceilings. Midge, the last to arrive, occupied the penthouse, where opportunities to inflict damage were few, until she discovered even better victims than members of her own species. Turning somersaults, she would entice the cats into jumping up on her cage, then run underneath to nip at their paws. Whenever I heard a cat yelp I knew she was playing another of her tricks.

Except for Midge, who was a youngster not yet fully grown, and the obviously elderly Gramps, I had no idea of how old the chipmunks were when they arrived. To whatever their ages might have been, an extraordinary six years was added for Gramps, and ten years for most of the others. Midge danced and turned somersaults until she was twelve. Then she built a nest.

I had given her a pot of earth, thinking she might enjoy digging in it, and so she did for a while. Then it became apparent that the digging was not just for fun any more. At a certain depth she began going around and around, trampling the earth down until she had fashioned a neat little bowl, and into the bowl she tamped down bits of the tissue and leaves I gave her for bedding. She was very fussy, searching among the leaves, sniffing and fingering, selecting only a few that were carefully shredded and pressed into the mold.

Working on the nest became an obsession. She no longer begged for nuts. She didn't even stop to eat. Even during the night I would hear her rustling around, working in the dark.

Finally she seemed satisfied. The completed bowl was a little masterpiece, beautifully molded, softly lined, just big enough for her to fit into. Late in the afternoon she tried it out, curled up in it, pulled a leaf over her for a cover, and was quiet. The next morning she was still there, and she was dead.

*W*AS THAT THE REASON for Pest's leaf gathering? Had he, like Midge, put them in a bowl to curl up in and not awaken? Or had the leaf gathering merely coincided with his luck running out, as it was bound to sooner or later? Had he finally encountered one of his many enemies, or tried to cross the road at the wrong moment, or — anyway, he was gone.

Yet somehow I couldn't believe he was gone, even after three weeks had passed. Whenever I went near the front door of his mansion, it seemed he would surely pop out and run over to greet me. One morning as I was carrying Squeak's milk to the barn, with Squeak accompanying me as usual, a flicker of movement caught my eye as we neared the doorway. It wasn't my imagination, because the tilt of Squeak's ears told me he had seen something, too. "Pest?" I called. We stood staring, and I thought the darkness in the doorway shifted slightly. Then all at once a little nose appeared, and a small head. The body emerged partway, and I saw that it was not Pest but a tiny replica, bright as a new penny. For a second it looked at us in utter disbelief. Then it dove back into the tunnel and disappeared.

Had Pest become a mother? Was he a she, and had we just seen one of her offspring? Had the bearing of young been the purpose of the leaf gathering, and did the rearing of a family account for the long absence? Although the relief this explanation gave me was no doubt disproportionate, nevertheless I felt a lifting of the spirit, as if the day had grown a little brighter.

But when another week passed and there still was no sign of her, hope that she was just busy caring for young ones began to wear thin. Chipmunks are far from devoted mothers. Once the babies acquire teeth they are presumed to be self-sufficient and are driven out of the den, to face unknown perils without guidance and find food and shelter as best they can. Soon we began to hear a lot of chipmunk trillings and chirpings, and once in a while we'd see a couple of youngsters darting about, no doubt trying to keep out of each other's way. It may have looked as though they were just having fun playing, but the game was probably deadly serious, for even at so tender an age chipmunks are inclined toward committing genocide.

At last I quite gave up hope of seeing Pest again, but then one day Squeak and I were sitting near the house and all at once something plopped down on him. He jumped, and I jumped, and whatever had startled us also jumped, then came to dance around my feet. It was Pest, bold as ever, demanding her three nuts, cramming them into her mouth, bounding off with them, and returning almost immediately for three more. Once again I had to admonish, "Don't walk over Squeak!" It was as if she had never been away.

That marked the beginning of the summer in which I traveled with three oddly assorted companions and everything was good, even the weather. It rained seldom, mostly at night and in moderation, just enough to keep foliage green and to prevent the brook from going dry. Thunderstorms were few and mild, distant rumblings with lightning flickering harmlessly in the sky. Wind only touched the trees gently, making their tops sway in ever-changing patterns against a bright blue sky. Each leaf and each blade of grass glistened with well-being.

Going out in the afternoon, I have only to call and Squeak is instantly at my side. Inside the barn Pixie thumps to her feet, joints stiffened with age moving somewhat reluctantly, and her hooves clatter over the floor to the door. She is no longer sure-footed enough to cross the rock bridge over the brook, so we go the other way, down the path toward the pasture. A freak storm at the end of May had burdened trees in almost full leaf with a heavy wet snow, and a little above the pasture a great old maple had fallen under the weight. The enormous trunk lies stretched out, shattered at its base, but, refusing to believe in death, it continues to send nourishment to its many branches that reach out with leaves still crisp and green.

We walk toward this stricken giant, the cat, the goat, and I, and before long our procession is joined by another small figure, a chipmunk erratically keeping us company like a wind-blown leaf, visible one minute, the next minute lost in a clump of bushes.

Pixie goes to work at once on the prostrate tree, plucking leaves from what had been the highest branches closest to the sun. I start cutting off lower branches that are dead or sparsely leafed and sawing them into transportable lengths. Squeak goes to a patch of sunlight and sits in it to wash an out-thrust leg, or rolls over to flip his body from side to side in the sandy soil. Pest skitters around my feet, climbs a leg, and gets suicidally close to the saw. I have as always taken the precaution of putting a supply of peanuts in my pockets, and with three of them bulging her cheeks, so that she looks as if she has come down with the mumps, she goes bounding up the hill. I must keep a wary eye out for her, though, because in about five minutes she is back and getting in the way again. However, the energy she needs to run up and down the hill is not limitless. After about six trips she is evidently worn out, and we see no more of her on that day.

Nor is my own energy limitless. After cutting one last big branch I put aside the saw, choose an uncluttered piece of ground to sit on, and Squeak joins me, collapsing in a single movement against my thigh. With my hand on his body I am aware of a certain kinship, and gazing up at the trees towering over us, their tips touching infinity, I feel that he and they are close to an acceptance of life that I should attain.

I have a friend, an unfortunate fellow who sees only flaws. Show him a beautiful garden and he is sure to find a weed in it. "Yes," he will say, "I suppose it might be pretty if it weren't for that weed." That, I realize on this summer's day, was the way I had been looking at life, concentrating on the weeds. I remember one miserable, cold, rainy day, when the roof leaked and a light fixture broke and the toilet overflowed and the mail contained nothing but rejected manuscripts, I said to myself, "No matter which way I turn, I can find nothing good to look at."

Samson was alive then, still running off with things stolen from my pockets and kicking up his heels as he raced with Pixie to the pasture. This tree that now lies here dying was still standing full of life. I had all about me these many other trees, old friends, and I had this small portion of earth, so full of beauty, for a home. And I could find nothing good to look at?

I glance down at Squeak and am aware of how much I need to learn.

"There are flaws in your life, too," I tell him. "Days without the sunlight that you love, days of rain and wind and bitter cold and snow. You take whatever comes without complaint, wait patiently for the air to warm and the sun to shine again. And when it does you abandon yourself to the enjoyment of this one day, this one hour, this minute, without memory of past discomforts or worry about those to come. This is what you must teach me, you who are only a cat, yet not a cat. How to accept, and endure, and then enjoy, with no thought of yesterday or tomorrow, a day like today, in which, no matter which way I look, I can find no flaw."

Over to our left, somewhere in the dense growth of saplings, a thrush begins to twitter. Like an opera singer getting in good voice for a concert, he tries out the twelve notes of his melody, goes through them again with a bit more assurance, then breaks into full song to announce the setting of the sun. It is time for us to go home.

Mention of the word brings Squeak instantly to his

feet, to stand by while I more clumsily get up on mine. I call to Pixie, who is on the other side of the fallen tree, just a glimmer of white seen through a mass of green leaves. "Time to go home," I tell her. She knows perfectly well what that means, but pretends she hasn't heard. Her back is toward us, and she goes on grazing as if not at all aware of our presence. But we have gone no more than ten paces when we hear her rustling through the leaves to catch up with us. So our procession, minus one small member who is accustomed to retiring early and may already be asleep deep down in her mansion, reverses itself and goes back up the hill toward the coming night.

As if in a speeded-up time machine, the days flash by, each one imperceptibly shorter. The leaves still left on the fallen maple tree droop and wither, and Pixie turns her attention to a nearby patch of succulent touch-me-nots, sending seeds popping in all directions as she moves among them. The earth begins to look a little dusty and shopworn, except on either side of our path down the hill, where wild asters and goldenrod put on a massive display of lavender and white and gold.

Then the fall rains come to make everything bright and clean again, but keep us indoors, Pixie in her half of the barn munching on hay, Squeak in his half, hunched resignedly on a burlap bag laid over the top of his barrel, I in the house taking care of odd jobs that had needed doing all summer, and Pest nowhere to be seen. She is such a foolish creature that I worry about her. Evidently having packed her mansion to overflowing, she had begun storing her nuts in a number of auxiliary dwellings scattered within a radius of fifty feet, and one of these is located on the bank of the brook that rain has turned into a fierce torrent, with foaming waterfalls and powerful rapids sending large boulders crashing downstream.

Banks on both sides are inundated. Water spills over Pest's burrow, and I fear she might have been so preoccupied with gloating over her wealth there that she failed to notice she was in danger until too late. My mind is on her as I slog through the mud toward the barn, with water dripping off the rain hat onto my nose, and apparently I cannot think of two things at the same time because I forget to duck, and tear right through the spider web that for many summers has occupied the upper half of the barn doorway. Afflicted as I am with arachnophobia so severe that I cannot so much as touch the page of a book containing a photo or even a drawing of a spider, I react now in sheer horror. I have often seen this particular spider, a bloated matriarch with long, furry legs, squatting at the center of her web like an empress surveying her realm. Was she there when I plunged my head into it? Is she somewhere on me now? As I desperately brush her threads off my face my breath comes fast and my heart pounds. If I do find her on me I'll surely die, or at least faint dead away.

Quite as strong as my fear of spiders, though, is my respect and even fondness for them. Naturalist Ivan Sanderson, a victim of the same phobia, had a novel explanation for this paradox. In very early days, he said, our forebears were members of a tribe that revered spiders, but, as was the custom among primitive peoples, initiation rites at the time of puberty included eating a specimen of the tribal fetish. Hence the combination of revulsion and something close to reverence. Whatever the explanation might be, I confound people by keening in agony at the close proximity of a spider, then fiercely averting any attempt to take its life. That's why I have for years bent almost double going through the barn doorway, as a rule so automatically that I continue to do so even during the early part of the winter, long after the spider has retired.

Later in the day I pay another visit to the barn and duck as usual, then with a great lurch of the heart am glad I did, because there's the spider, very visible and very active, constructing a new web. I watch fascinated, with chills going down my spine. Can spiders count? She draws a thread from the center to the perimeter, walks five steps, draws another thread back to the center, returns to the perimeter and takes five more steps. Always five steps. I send thoughts to her, telling her I'm sorry I destroyed her web, promising I'll be more careful from now on, and because I've given my word, but mostly because knowing she is directly overhead is exquisite torture, I almost crawl on hands and knees going in through the doorway this time.

Not long afterward the rain stops, and it is almost as if a plug has been pulled, the water in the brook goes down so fast. Whitecaps and waterfalls disappear, banks reappear, the angry roar subsides to a busy rippling. Standing just outside the barn I feel something nudge against my leg, and there is Pest. She had not been trapped inside the flooded burrow. I am so pleased to see her that I start laughing, and that brings Squeak out of the barn. As if just to please him, sunlight suddenly appears, and he goes to sit in it, to watch while Pest takes her three nuts and bounds off to deposit them. I call to Pixie, and to celebrate the return of the sun we troop down the hill, Squeak and Pixie fastidiously picking their way around puddles, I in my already soaked shoes splashing through them without caring.

LD-TIMERS CALL such autumn downpours "line rains," because they occur around the time of the equinox and usually bring about an abrupt change in temperature. So it was this time. Nights turned cold, brittle with frost. Days were crisp and dazzling under cloudless skies, with the air so thin that a shout seemed to go through it like a hurled knife.

All during the days and the nights whispering leaves left the trees and floated down. Touching the ground, they pattered like little feet, even fooling Squeak into a quick turn of the head to see who might be approaching. Both of us disliked the noise we made shuffling through them. If the wind swept a clear channel, he would make a detour so that he could tread silently. I raked paths to the barn, the mouse cage, and the road. Pest made fewer trips to get nuts, either because she finally became aware of a surplus, although such a cessation of greed seemed unlikely, or, more likely, because even so foolhardy a creature must have realized that the leaves made her passage more hazardous. We saw less and less of her, until she appeared only once in the morning, to greet me when I first went outside.

But where the wind piled leaves the highest, Pixie ploughed through happily, sounding as if she were as big as an elephant, ingesting as indiscriminately as a vacuum cleaner at first, but growing increasingly selective as the supply became more abundant. Even after watching her for days I could not understand her way of choosing, rejecting the most delectable-looking reds and saffrons to eagerly lip in dried-up brown ones that crumbled in her mouth.

Winter came abruptly, much too early, taking us unawares, Pixie and Squeak without their winter coats, me without having put up storm windows and the banking around the house. On a gloomy afternoon a cold, sullen rain started falling, and clouds rolled in so close to the ground that I had to grope in premature darkness to feed Pixie. From what was probably a necessary trip, Squeak arrived in his part of the barn dripping wet, and since my jacket was also soaked our conference that evening was less a pleasure than a mutual commiseration. Shortly after I returned to the house the wind-driven patter of rain against the windowpanes changed to a peculiar swishing and tapping, like minuscule fingers asking for admittance. The rain had changed to sleet. And a little later there was a heavy silence that was in itself a sound, the hush of falling snow.

The next morning we woke in a different world, closed in by branches weighed down with snow that hung like curtains, and young trees bent under loads, touching their tops to the ground. Sounds were muffled, as if the air had thickened so that they could not get through. Whatever might be happening outside this small, white-walled enclosure could be neither seen nor heard.

I shoveled snow away from one barn door to free Pixie, from the other to free Squeak, and poured hot water over the door of the mouse cage to melt the ice that had frozen it shut. Then later, after all of us had been fed, came the big job of the day — digging out of the snow one of the logs from the pile just in front of the barn, dragging it inside, and cutting it into firewood. Perched on top of his barrel, Squeak watched me working through half-closed eyes. Pixie came in to stand beside me and press her head against my leg, nosing in closer and closer to the blade of the saw until I said, "You're a nuisance," gave her a handful of peanuts, and told her to go away.

Toward evening a wind came up, and by nightfall such a gale was blowing that I had to walk backward to the barn to give Pixie her dinner, and again to confer with and feed Squeak. All through the night the house creaked and shuddered as blasts slammed against its north side, and clumps of snow dislodged from the trees thundered on the roof. The temperature went down below zero and stayed there for three days, while the wind continued its assault. Then on the fourth day, the sun shone, the air was quiet, the trees shook off what snow remained on their branches and sprang upright, the roof of the house dripped icicles, and snowslides roared down off the steeply sloping barn roof, terrifying the occupants so that Squeak shot out of his doorway and Pixie tumbled out of hers, and I gave thanks that I had not been passing by at that moment.

The thaw lasted long enough to flood the goat yard and the paths, and turn the brook into a broad lake of water sliding over and under sheets of ice. Then the temperature plummeted to below zero again and everything froze, including the water pipes in the house. I thawed them out with the electric iron, chopped ice away from both entrances to the barn, again used boiling water to unfreeze the door to the mouse cage. Sharp reports like gunshots sounded here and there throughout the woods, as ice in the crevices of trees split them open. Nearer at hand, the brook suddenly exploded. Choked by thick ice, it rumbled like a volcano readying for an eruption, gave a mighty belch, and burst open. A miniature geyser shot up, froze practically in midair, and around the site of the rupture, welts rose like scar tissue, with water trickling out and turning almost immediately into little fingers of ice. Like some menacing substance in a horror movie the fingers gradually bulged and elongated, and sent out tentacles that crept in all directions, even uphill and over barricades. They slid over the sill and insinuated through the wire of the mouse cage, where they merged and spread to form a thick, smothering sheet of ice. They sent feelers toward the house and into the barn, and when I chopped them off, water oozed from the severed ends to form new fingers. Slowly they advanced toward Pest's mansion, and I hacked desperately to keep them from going through her doorway. I was losing the battle when snow started falling, and kept on falling all through the day until the ground was covered with a three-foot blanket under which the ice in turn was finally smothered.

Before there were snowplows to open the roads, farmers used to drive their horses back and forth, trampling down the snow to make a surface hard and smooth enough for their wagons to go over. I put on high boots and emulated a horse, ploughing through the drifts and walking back and forth to make paths that were more like canyons, leading to the two barn doors and to the mouse cage. Squeak padded up and down the canyons, searching for a way to get to one of his secluded areas, until urgency forced him to use the middle of a path, where he dug a hole deep enough to accommodate half a dozen deposits, then vigorously raked snow from all sides to make sure it was properly filled in. Pixie ventured out of the barn, sank into a drift, and floundered wildly, her cry of protest muffled by a mouthful of snow.

Still more snow fell, and a fierce wind piled it in drifts that defied scaling. With an ax I cut steps up one side and down the other, trampling each step until it was smooth and almost as hard as rock. Squeak followed as I worked, staying so close that if I backed up suddenly I almost fell over him. Pixie, having learned her lesson, left the barn only twice a day, when I forced her into taking a short excursion to eat her grain. Lack of exercise made her put on weight, and her hooves grew so that they began to turn up like Oriental slippers. Each day I worked on them, as long as my hands could stand the cold, to file them down.

All year round there are the same number of hours in a day, the same seven days in a week, the same number of days, give or take one, in a month. Why, then, should time pass so swiftly in summer that it seems to have only begun when it is gone, and so slowly in winter that the end is like a mirage that one plods toward but never reaches?

Imprisoned not by steel bars but by icy winds and

deep snow, I marked off the days of January and February, the two worst months of winter, but March, usually graced with a few days giving a hint of spring, offered no respite. Shivering had become as constant as breathing, and trudging through snow had so altered my gait that I doubted I'd ever walk normally again. Squeak's had also changed, but for a different reason. He had put on so much fat as insulation against the cold that he waddled like an overstuffed goose. Nevertheless, he shivered so that when he sat hunched on his burlap bag while I cut wood I could see his head shaking, and during our evening conference he could not stop trembling, nor could I. So even though he clung to me, not wanting me to leave, I made my stay brief in the hope that he would get warmed up in his barrel of hay as I would, at last, in the house.

Toward the middle of March, Pixie's health declined alarmingly. She lost interest in food. I had to push her out of the barn and lead her to her grain and almost beg her to eat. The heavy winter coat made her still look plump, but if I thrust my fingers through the thick wool I could feel her ribs and the sharp ridge of her spine. Finally one morning I found her lying stretched out, responding when I spoke to her only with the slight flick of an ear. The right side of her body was icy cold, and so stiff that I couldn't even make the legs bend. She had had a stroke.

I gave her some vodka, which she lapped up willingly, massaged her legs to coax life back into them, and as soon as they were warmer I pulled her to her feet. At once a veritable flood poured out of her. Either she hadn't been able to empty her bladder lying down, or else she had been reluctant to soil herself. After that she seemed to brighten a bit, and she struggled to stay on her feet. The legs on the left side supported her well enough, the right ones sagged, and down she went in a heap. Her eyes followed me as I walked toward the door, and she whimpered when I left, but I was back soon with a bucket of warm water that she drank eagerly, taking in almost as much as she had just eliminated. Then she closed her eyes and slept, and when she woke late in the afternoon it was time to be cruel to her.

Muscles deteriorate rapidly. To reduce the crippling effect of the stroke she had to be moved about as much as possible, as soon as possible. I pulled her to her feet and tried to make her stand. She slumped down. I pulled her up again. She slumped again. She was heavy and I was too out of breath for a third try, but an hour later I returned and lifted her once more, and this time she stayed up, swaying, her legs trembling violently. She tried to walk and collapsed, thrashed around until I helped her to her feet again, took a few shuffling steps, sagged, pulled herself up and took a few more steps, her eyes on the feed dish

I had brought in and left on the floor. She was hungry. A good sign.

In the early darkness Squeak was waiting for me when I left the barn. Staying close to my feet, he walked with me all the way to the door of the house, and when I came out again with a flashlight and Pixie's grain, he was still there, waiting to accompany me back to the barn.

"I'll be with you in just a little while," I told him. "As soon as Pixie has had her dinner."

While she was busy eating, leaning against the wall for support, I had time to clean up her bed and give her fresh hay. Her appetite had returned. It was almost as if the stroke had acted as a purge. She ate all the grain, licked the dish to make sure she had not missed a single kernel, then fell down. I lifted her and helped her back to bed, adjusted the paralyzed legs so that she was in a comfortable position, and tucked a blanket around her.

It was long past time for Squeak's dinner. I told him I'd bring it out almost immediately, and as if he understood he didn't follow me back to the house this time, but went toward his part of the barn. Then it turned out that what he wanted was not so much food as reassurance. When I put down the plate he simply stood at my feet, waiting. We hadn't had our conference.

All the unaccustomed lifting had made every muscle in my body ache so that it actually felt good to sit down for a while. I stroked him and talked to him, trying to sort out my thoughts.

"She's very old. Do you know how old she is? Almost eighteen. It's time for her to go, and I must not try to keep her. But it doesn't seem fair, her having gone through such a hard winter and then not being allowed to enjoy the spring. That's what I wish for her, all I wish for, that she can stay here just a little while longer, just until the earth turns green."

Once the conference routine had been observed Squeak was, after all, very hungry. When I said it was time for me to go home he jumped up with alacrity and went to his plate. Yet after one hasty bite he had to stop and look up at me, reminding me of the last step of our ritual, a good-night pat on the head.

A newborn day is a robber of energy. From each of us it sucks vitality, so that in the early morning life is at its lowest ebb, the cessation of life at its peak. I slept for a few hours, and just at dawn went out to the barn. In the eerie half-light I could see Pixie lying on her side, legs stretched out full length, head extended, and my mind leaped back to that other dawn in which I had seen Samson's body in that same position. I spoke to Pixie. There was no response. I lifted her head. It fell back. I cried out her name, and she woke with a start, to stare at me sleepily.

Relief made me laugh, and startled out of a deep

sleep in which she had been dreaming who knows what, she must have thought she should respond to my laughter as she had in her youth, with a merry caper. Her legs thrashed wildly.

Goats have a peculiar way of rising. The back goes up first, putting them momentarily in a most ungainly, downright ludicrous, pose, upright on their hind legs, forelegs still folded under. In the second stage the forelegs are unfolded to heave up the front end, and what had begun to look like the impossible is accomplished. They are standing.

Almost never are goats found lying flat on their sides, no doubt because scrambling to their feet from this position would be difficult for quite healthy individuals. Pixie couldn't manage without my help. First I tucked in her front legs and rolled her over to put them under her. Hooking my fingers into her hip bones to get a good grip, I tugged with all my might while she fought to get up on her hind legs. Then somehow she had to unfold and stand on the good front one. At last she succeeded, but was so thrown off balance by the effort that she stumbled forward until her head hit the wall with a thud. Somehow I managed to grab her before she fell again. Then the two of us stood panting, incapable of doing anything more for a while.

She had lain without moving far too long. When I tried to make her walk she shuffled only a few steps and started to sag. I put a rope around her neck to hold her up, and with a hand on her flank to keep her from tipping over, I led her around until she had limbered up. And that became a ritual we followed from then on.

Every morning at dawn I went to the barn, woke her and pulled her to her feet, put a rope around her neck, and led her close to the walls of the barn around and around, counting the turns, one, two, three, four, and a fifth that was all she had strength for. At first she was puzzled. Going nowhere like that must have seemed like a ridiculous expenditure of energy that was already in short supply. Then she became obstinate. I had to almost carry her around the turns. But when I remained firm she changed her tactics and thought of all kinds of diversions. She had to stop for a drink of water. She had to look in her feed dish to make sure it contained no grain. Wasn't there one kernel left in it, or one on the floor beside the dish? Then she absolutely had to stop and chew on her salt block for a while. But persistence eventually turned the routine into a habit, and as such it became so automatic that I didn't have to lead her around any more. She made the rounds all by herself, much like a circus horse in the ring, while I played ringmaster counting the turns, "One, two, three, four, five. That's it. Now you can go to bed."

Gratefully she headed for her stall, but stopped short of going in, because she knew there was a piece of apple in my pocket. "If you want the apple you must go all the way in," I told her, and she lurched forward until her nose touched the wall. "Now turn around," I said. This was difficult because the paralyzed foot caught in the bedding. It had to be done in small stages and took a while, but at last she was facing me, her eyes on the pocket. I praised her and gave her the apple and waited to make sure she was lying down comfortably. Then in the harsh light of the rising sun I gratefully headed back to my own bed.

A day of freezing rain put a thick crust of ice on the snow. Squeak was no longer restricted to traveling on the paths. He could go anywhere, and I could go nowhere without gyrating wildly to stay on my feet. I spilled his milk, flung away most of Pixie's grain, somehow managed to plunge almost my entire arm into her water bucket.

The day after that the sun shone, and the glitter on the world of ice was almost blinding. Every tree down to the smallest branch was made of crystal that sent out sparkling rays of red and blue and green. Twigs tinkled against each other like glass chimes, then crashed together in stronger gusts of wind that shattered their ice coatings and sent chunks clattering to the ground, a steady bombardment that made walking anywhere hazardous for Squeak and unpleasant for me, with icy fragments sliding under my coat collar and swiftly turning to ice water trickling down my back. All through the woods there was a constant din of crackling and falling ice, with an occasional louder crash as a weakened, overweighted branch splintered and fell.

But the sun brought warmth, and, as old-timers used to say, the snow began to rot. Hard crusts of ice broke up, and what was underneath turned soft. Taken by surprise, Squeak gave a fine display of consternation followed by outrage, as he broke through where he had walked confidently on the surface the previous day, and in trying to get back to solidity only sank deeper still. My paths that had been trampled smooth and hard unexpectedly gave way underfoot, not at every step, but unpredictably, so that once again I was constantly losing balance. Then an overnight freeze turned every indentation made the day before into a hazardous pothole, and going anywhere at all became almost impossible.

Day by day the landscape we had got used to was altered as the snow gradually subsided. The tops of cars passing on the road became visible. The handle of a rake, lost all winter, poked out of a drift. Remnants of the woodpile that had been buried reappeared. A round piece of metal, discovered in the middle of a path, was two days later identified as the bottom of an upturned bucket. On a hillock in front of the barn a small brown patch appeared, an ugly scar in the white snow, a beautiful, beautiful thing to see, earth, bare earth, evidence that under the winter's rotting, spring lay waiting to be born.

I spread a burlap bag on the brown patch and Squeak and I sat on it, two ludicrous figures on an island in a sea of snow. He shivered, but with pleasure rather than cold, I thought, and I talked to him.

"The snow is melting fast. With some luck it should be gone soon. Grass will begin to grow and buds will appear on the trees. Pixie will have something green to eat, after so many months of nothing but dry hay. That's all I ask for, that she can have that pleasure for just a little while, a few weeks, maybe, or even just a few days."

S PRING WAS LATE in arriving. At the end of April, snow still lay on the ground. When Squeak and I tried to walk in the woods where sunlight couldn't penetrate, we were turned back by drifts still almost knee-high. Although tree trunks were tinged faintly with the blush of rising sap, their branches were still quite bare of buds. But Pixie was gaining in strength.

"Hold on," I told her. "We're almost there. You know how spring is. It comes all at once. One morning we'll wake up and the earth will be green. There'll be all kinds of good things for you to eat."

I chopped away patches of ice that remained on the path outside the barn, looped a rope around her neck, and led her out. She wobbled and was frightened until I put a hand on her flank to steady her. Then she walked well enough, around the side of the barn and out a little way toward the road. While she stood looking at this world that had been alien to her for so many months, I searched the nearby ground. All I could find were a few very short blades of grass and some tiny wild aster leaves, less than a mouthful. She lipped them in eagerly and begged for more, but I went everywhere and came back empty-handed.

The next day she left the barn willingly, caught her bad foot on a protruding rock, swiveled around, and fell down. She had become used to taking sudden tumbles, though, and also to being helped back on her feet. Calmly she waited until I came to lift her hindquarters, then with some thrashing managed to get up on her front legs. She shuffled around, picking up a few dry leaves that evidently were not too unpalatable, while I hunted everywhere and found nothing green. Yet it seemed to me there was a change in the appearance of treetops silhouetted against the sky. Was I only wishing them there, or were tiny buds forming? "Soon," I told Pixie. "Soon."

The following morning I went outside and stood transfixed, hardly believing what I saw. Pixie had left the barn voluntarily and had walked a short distance all by herself. In a patch of sunlight she was sitting with forelegs neatly tucked under, head raised toward the warmth of the sun, eyes half-closed. And nearby, in another patch of sunlight, Squeak sat in precisely the same pose, forelegs tucked under, head lifted, eyes closed against the sun's brightness. It was a scene of such friendliness and tranquility that I hated to spoil it with my entrance.

The day after that it rained, heavily, steadily. Squeak broke a strict rule. Instead of going some distance away and out of sight, he squatted near the barn and hastened back in again, to sit on top of his barrel and wash himself dry, then stare pensively through the open door at the downpour. Pixie didn't stir from her stall but remained on her feet, a good sign, and contentedly munched on hay. I was the only one truly discomfited. By late afternoon, after having made trips to give Pixie her breakfast and Squeak his milk, to carry out Pixie's water and carry in several loads of firewood, I had soaked through five pairs of shoes and had each chair in the house draped with a dripping jacket.

More tired than usual, I overslept the next morning and would have been late in getting to the barn if dawn itself hadn't been more than half an hour late. It was gray and soggy and cold, but at least the rain had stopped. With crackers and a piece of apple in my pocket and a cheery good-morning ready to be spoken, I peered into Pixie's still dark stall. She was lying on her side with her legs stretched out. When I bent over her she raised her head and cried. She had had another stroke.

This time she hadn't been able to wait and had

wet her bed. I lifted her enough to tuck dry hay under, then offered the crackers and apple, and she took them so eagerly that I went back into the house to get more. On the way I noticed bitterly a shimmer of green on the ground. The rain had accelerated growth. Grass was beginning to come up. Too late.

It couldn't be too late. I wouldn't allow it to be too late. I tore a wide strip from a sheet, knelt down beside Pixie, and managed to work one end of it under her body to pull it through on the other side, making a kind of sling around her belly, just above the hips. Then I put another strip around her neck, gave a mighty heave on both at the same time, and lifted her to her feet. Gratefully she relieved herself of a lot of little chocolate marbles. With the toe of my shoe I pushed them to one side so she wouldn't lie on them when she went down. She tried to get her legs more firmly under her. They trembled and buckled. She straightened them. They sagged and she went halfway down. She straightened them again and pulled herself up. Her determination matched mine.

In his part of the barn, on the other side of the wall, Squeak was snoring. Evidently he slept so heavily that all the noise Pixie and I made failed to arouse him. But now we were quiet, resting, standing side by side, her body leaning heavily against mine. I eased up on the sling. She remained standing. I tried slowly easing myself away from her, and she toppled over.

"Never mind," I said. "Sleep for a while. We'll try again later."

Close to the horizon the sun glittered through the trees. Groggy and stiff with cold, I returned to the house and crawled into bed to sleep for a couple of hours. Then the regular day began, and although Pixie couldn't stand unaided, she seemed a little stronger.

As I'd predicted, spring came with a rush. Suddenly the earth was green. Buds appeared on the trees, unfolded, and became leaves so swiftly that it was almost like watching a time-lapse film. I put the slings around Pixie's belly and neck and half-carried her out of the barn so that she could at least look at this bright new landscape. Nearby, Squeak stood watching, staring at Pixie, a puzzled look in his eyes. She shuffled around, taking the short steps of the infirm, went toward the sunlight slanting through the trees, and stood in it. I took away the sling and she remained standing.

Now Squeak was staring at me, and I realized that in talking to Pixie I had mentioned the word *walk*. As soon as I moved away from her, he started toward the brook, turned to look back, then stood waiting for me. I broke a few branches from a maple tree and gave them to Pixie so she could chew on the young leaves, told her we wouldn't be gone long, and crossed the bridge with Squeak leading the way.

At last we could check on what damage the fierce winter winds might have done in the woods, always a suspenseful mission, but a happy one this time. At least in the woodlot no trees had fallen, nor even any very large branches, and with relief I saw that once again the old hemlock had been spared. A giant towering over all the others, it was so ancient that I could imagine its having witnessed the passage of Indians when the land was theirs, and I often wondered what miracle had caused it to be overlooked by the tanners when their axes had so devastated the surrounding forests.

Sometimes I would take visitors back into the woods to show them this tree and ask if they could see anything unusual about it. Most stared at it and prowled around and shook their heads. Apart from the great height and girth, it seemed to them in no way different from its neighbors. But occasionally someone would notice the path going up one side. Hidden in the densely needled branches near the top there was a hollow in which many generations of raccoons had been born and raised, and the bark on the one side had been worn smooth by years and years of traffic to and from that hollow.

Always in early spring and late in the fall I paid a visit to this hemlock, in the spring to make sure it had got through the winter safely, in the fall to wish it well during the winter to come. On this day I put my arms as far as they would go around its trunk and laid my cheek against the side where the bark was worn smooth. It is said that when some native tribes wish to clear a wooded area, they kill unwanted trees by continuously cursing and beating them. In reverse, then, a caress and a kind word might prolong the life of this old friend.

From the hemlock we went down the hill a little way to say hello to another old friend, an enormous rock with a young maple tree and a profusion of rock fern growing on its flat top. A thick mat of bright green moss cascaded down three of its sides. The fourth was sculptured in waves, undercut probably many centuries ago by the strong current of a stream that had flowed past. Exposed in the undercut were many different-colored layers to show how the rock had been born at the bottom of a lake or an ocean, perhaps as far back in time as when the earth itself had been born, each layer an accumulation of hundreds of years of silt turned by pressure into stone. Staring at that ancient rock put us in proper perspective. Just as countless lives had been buried in each of these layers of silt, so ours eventually would be in another layer, to become part of an object of wonder and conjecture for future lives that would, in their turn, become silt.

As we climbed back up the hill Squeak stopped often to sit down for a moment. Either the walk had tired him after so many months of inactivity, or, more likely, he was trying to remind me that it was customary for us to pause in our walk for a conference. The ground was still wet and the only rock I could find was not very satisfactory, somewhat tilted and hardly big enough for the two of us. He managed to fit himself into the small space beside me, almost at once started slowly sliding down, got up to make an adjustment, and immediately started sliding again. Besides, even through my heavy slacks I could feel in the rock the stored-up winter's chill.

"Let's go home," I said, and he agreed instantly.

Pixie was no longer standing. For a heart-stopping moment I couldn't see her at all, she was lying so flat, but as soon as she caught sight of us she started thrashing, flailing her legs so wildly that she actually drove her body around in circles. "Wait," I called to her, and at once she was quiet. Her eyes followed me as I went to pick up her slings, and when I brought them she tried to help by lifting her body a little so one could be slipped under her. "Up!" I said, and both of us heaved with such fine coordination that she was at once on her feet, making a great show of being unperturbed by picking up and chewing on a leaf, maybe to cover the embarrassment over her loss of dignity.

"We must not leave her alone like that any more," I told Squeak.

The days warmed. I changed to a lighter jacket,

and finally to a sleeveless vest with pockets in it, a necessary part of my attire no matter how hot it might get, because I had to take a supply of peanuts with me wherever I went. Each afternoon I would go to the barn and give Pixie a few, then put the slings around her belly and her neck, and we'd go for a walk, with Squeak always keeping us company, stopping politely whenever we stopped, advancing as we advanced. We moved in a world of gleaming wonder, with new green everywhere so tender that it almost made the heart ache, so full of vigor that it made the spirit soar. I could feel Pixie responding, absorbing strength from this abundance of new life.

But now I began to worry about Squeak. He had acquired a bad cough, I thought because he spent so much of his time sitting or lying on the ground still soggy from the seepage of ice melting beneath the surface. He had his bed in the barn and his barrel outside the barn, but almost always I'd find him stationed in front where he had a clear view of comings and goings and could be ready instantly if Pixie and I started out for a walk.

I found a heavy cardboard box and placed it bottom up in this favorite spot of his, but he would have nothing to do with it. I put his breakfast milk and some dry chow on it. He hastily drank the milk, ignored the chow, hopped off, and settled down on the ground a few feet away from the box. I did some thinking, remembered how he always accepted the burlap bag no matter where it was put, and tried draping it over the box. His response was instantaneous. Testing the box with a paw to make sure of its solidity, he jumped up on it, sat down, and purred. I gave him the dish of food he had spurned, and he ate. Then after the obligatory face washing, he sat looking this way and that, enjoying the view in dry comfort.

From then on he spent most of the day on the box. In case of rain I had to take it in at night, but first thing in the morning I put it out, and with his breakfast served on it his appetite was greatly improved. In fact it increased astoundingly. When I went out again after I'd had my own breakfast the chow was always gone. I gave him second and third helpings. He never showed any immediate interest, yet when I checked a while later the dish would be empty again.

At last it occurred to me that he wasn't eating all that food. Somebody else was. Pretending to be busy working in the barn so that he would not feel duty bound to join me, I kept watch. He ate about half the chow and was sitting near it when I saw a tiny head poke out of a small tunnel under his outside barrel. After a quick look around, a deer mouse eased out, darted over to the box, climbed up the burlap bag, passed under Squeak's nose, hopped into the dish to snatch up a piece of the chow, hopped out, scrambled down the burlap bag, and disappeared in the tunnel.

As the mouse had slipped under his nose Squeak's head had jerked slightly, and he had watched with mild interest this initial raid on his food, but to subsequent visits of the mouse, which continued until the dish was empty, he paid no attention.

The mouse had not shown a trace of fear, just as Pest, and in the early days the birds, had not. What was there about Squeak that inspired such confidence? Certain of our emotions — fear, anger, and possibly lust — are betrayed, it is said, by the way we smell. Did Squeak exude an odor of tolerance? Or did these small creatures perceive what I could only feel, that somehow he actually wasn't a cat?

NE MORNING as I was putting Pixie's grain into her dish I felt a half-forgotten, instantly remembered bumping against my leg. There was Pest, alive, climbing toward a pocket. She had got through the hard winter safely. Now she took up exactly where she had left off months before, demanding her three nuts, one for each cheek pouch and one to carry in her mouth.

Pixie was busy lapping up her grain and took no notice, but Squeak's ears came forward as he watched Pest clambering up and down and darting away. Perhaps he had missed her, too, and was glad to see her.

So beyond expectations we were all together again, and at once hope reached out to consider another prospect. Far, far away, an impossible distance away, the lush green of the pasture shone in the sunlight, with

Squeak's big flat rock standing out almost white, as if bleached by the winter's snows. An unreachable goal? We could try.

In Pixie's eyes I had become omnipotent. There was nothing I could not do. Sometimes in the morning I would find her down on her side, with bedding pushed all in a heap, showing how she had struggled in futile efforts to get to her feet, and she would whimper an appeal to me with complete trust in her eyes. Even though the struggle that ensued was difficult for both of us, she was so sure I would succeed that as soon as she was on her feet she would calmly nibble on hay, while I slumped against a wall weak-kneed and out of breath.

Nor did she ever question my decisions. Putting the sling under her belly and a rope around her neck meant she was supposed to walk, and walk she did as best she could, in fits and starts and near-tumbles that jerked the rope and the sling every which way, making it almost impossible for me to keep my footing. Indeed, sometimes I headed for a fall and she supported me, instead of the other way around.

We always went the same way, toward the distant pasture. She came to know all the obstacles, each jutting rock and protruding root, and would carefully shuffle around them to put most of them in my way. Going up a slope was managed well enough, but going down terrified her. On the well-worn path there was one stretch I called Bugaboo Hill, because it gave us so much trouble. She would stand at the top of it trying to work up courage, lifting one foot and the other as if jogging in place, then take the plunge so recklessly that her body got ahead of her feet and she ended up quite literally in a nose dive. The rope and the sling dragged me down with her, and lying there side by side we were for an instant not a goat and a human, but two beings looking into each other's eyes to discover a common identity.

Day after day we went through that crisis, with Squeak standing at a safe distance, waiting for us to recover and go on. Each day we went a little farther. We were a third of the way there, halfway there, two thirds. I urged Pixie on until she began to pant and stumble, then untied the rope and removed the sling and told her she could rest. She knew there were good things in my pockets to reward her, and she could have snatched them out, but she waited politely to have them handed to her: a slice of bread, a graham cracker, a leaf of cabbage, a piece of apple. I warned her to take care not to fall over, then looked for a place to sit nearby, sometimes on a rock that was big enough, but mostly just a patch of ground not too cluttered with twigs and stones, and Squeak joined me.

It would have been pleasant to spend the whole day there idling through the hours, but there was work to be done. Reluctantly the word *home* was spoken, and after a last look to make sure Pixie was all right, we started back up the hill. As long as I remained outside, Squeak stayed with me. But as soon as I was in the house I would stand at the window and watch, and in a little while I'd see him trotting down the hill again, to spend the day not exactly with Pixie, but somewhere close by. He was always there when I went down with the rope and sling to take her home, and just as he had accompanied us in the morning he would return with us in the evening, keeping in step, waiting whenever Pixie had to stop to rest for a while.

The summer was as dry as the previous one had been, with almost no rain except at night. Days were warm, sometimes too warm for any expenditure of energy, but I'd give Pixie a cooling sponge bath before we started out, and we'd go a little way off the path to stop where there was shade under the big maple trees. One day I realized she had gained enough in strength so that the support of the rope around her neck was no longer needed, but the lame hind leg still made her swivel around and lose balance, and we had to keep on using the sling. In the morning her eyes would brighten as soon as she saw me take it off the hook. She had begun to enjoy our walks together and was eager to start out. Perhaps she had even become aware of our ultimate goal, and was longing to reach it.

We were almost there. We spent several sultry days

just outside the fence, where she browsed in the heavy brush while Squeak and I lolled on the dry leaves that had accumulated over the years. Then on a day that seemed just right, with a gentle breeze blowing and puffy clouds in the sky dappling the ground with drifting patches of shadow, I guided her through the gate.

We had reached Arcadia.

Squeak ran ahead to leap onto his big flat rock and stood waiting for me. Pixie walked with little mincing steps, one leg dragging, over the ground where she and Samson had once wandered and raced and crashed their heads together in mock battles. She tested a sprig of clover and found it good to eat and settled down to grazing. I went to the big rock and slid into the slight concavity where my body had always fitted so comfortably, and Squeak flung himself down beside me, got up, and flung himself down again, just for the pleasure of it. I rested a hand on his body to feel the throb of his purring and gazed at Pixie gleaming white in the sunlight, and it was almost as good as last summer, but not quite. Pixie couldn't make the trip unaided, and Pest was not with us any more.

Early in June she had gone around gathering leaves, then had disappeared, I presumed to give birth again. I missed her morning greeting and looked forward to her return, but three weeks passed, and four, and there was no sign of her. Often my eyes would play tricks on me, and I'd think I had seen her flitting in the path ahead of me, but it would be only a leaf stirred by a momentary breeze. Or I'd think I felt her climbing my leg, and find I had just brushed against a branch or a twig. Finally there were reminders of her everywhere, any number of chipmunks darting about so swiftly and erratically that I couldn't begin to make an accurate count, but not one came over to climb my leg. They all fled at the sight of me. No doubt they were Pest's babies. But where was she?

When she appeared at last I had got so used to not seeing her that she took me completely by surprise. "Why, Pest!" I almost shouted, and I was glad I had on the vest with peanuts in the pockets. She hesitated, staring at me as if not sure that I really remembered her, then climbed my leg and took a nut, but only one. Her fur was rumpled and had lost its shine, and I thought I detected some lack of agility in the way she returned to the ground. I called to her, offering another nut, but my voice seemed to fall short of reaching her, as if stopped by an invisible barrier. She didn't come back, nor did she go away. Sitting on a nearby rock she stuffed the single nut into one cheek pouch, took it out and shoved it into the other, took it out again and stared at it, then put it between her teeth, closed her eyes, and seemed to fall asleep. Even my moving about didn't disturb her. For a while she remained like that, then she opened her eyes to stare at the nut again, put it back between her teeth, and wandered around as if she didn't know what to do with it. At last she dug a hole in the ground, as I'd seen squirrels do but never a chipmunk, placed the nut in the hole, scraped a few leaves over it, and slipped away. And that was the last time we saw her.

*T*HEY WERE JEWEL DAYS, those days we spent in Arcadia.

"I'm putting them in a treasure chest," I told Squeak. "When dark days come I can take them out and look at them, and they'll still be sparkling. I must remember then that they are there."

While Pixie searched out sprigs of Quaker lady and clover and daisies and other things she liked to eat, we walked about in the pasture, and there was always something new for us to look at: a clump of Christmas fern half-hidden under old leaves at the foot of a tree; out-of-season white violets, supposed to bloom only in early spring, yet there they were; sexton beetles giving decent burial to a furry casualty I did not try to identify; a snake startled out of sun-warmed slumber slithering off through the grass; a newly built ant-hill swarming with activity. We stopped here to watch all the comings and goings, and as usual I could make no sense of the endless circling and traveling up and down, although I supposed it had some purpose. Then I had to brush off several ants making a surely purposeless trip up through Squeak's fur, and we turned away, back to our rock, to sit and appreciate for a while the goodness of the day.

Gradually the intense heat of summer waned. Sunlight came slanting a little farther from the south each day. All over the pasture, crickets started chirping, warning, "Winter is coming, winter is coming," and in the nearby woods chipmunks chattered endlessly, having a last noisy fling at defying fate before going underground for their long sleep. High overhead, beyond sight, the lonely cries of geese sped toward the south. Fluffs of down from gone-to-seed thistles and goldenrod floated through the air. The tips of ferns turned brown and crumbled to the touch. The great old maples circling the pasture shaded to a darker green, all except one that blazed with color as intense as the rays of the setting sun. I gave this one my pity, knowing the premature change foretold its death.

"But what a splendid way to die," I said to Squeak. "Not whimpering in protest, but shouting compliance. No stinking decay of the flesh, but a sweet-smelling turning from brilliance into dust. Wouldn't it be good if we could go that way? Or, better still, if we could just walk out of life, if I could say to you and Pixie,

'Come, let's go,' and we'd start out as we do to come down here, walking down the hill, then just keep on going, away and away and away. Yes, I'd like that. Even if it meant walking into nothing, in that instant of becoming nothing I think I'd be content if we were together."

How much did he understand, or sense, or feel? He listened, and I told him about the sultan's words.

"A long time ago this sultan whose name was Murad said, 'Those who study philosophy rightly, study to die.' I have followed that precept, and in these two summers, last summer and this one just coming to an end, I have studied well, I believe. I have learned that in a universe so immense that it extends far beyond our comprehension, worldly success must be meaningless, ambition foolish, possessions useless. Strip all that away, and what's in the small core of life that remains? For me, nothing much but a wish, an impossible wish, that we might stay together."

Of course an impossible wish.

As the trees celebrated the changing of seasons by tossing from their branches showers of multicolored leaves, day by day Pixie grew stronger and more agile. She didn't need me any longer. She could walk by herself, ploughing with confidence through piles of fallen leaves concealing all the pitfalls and obstacles that hitherto had made her lose her footing. With great determination, as if she had been thinking about making the trip for a long time and had finally decided this was the day, she crossed the brook one morning, picking her way carefully over and among the rocks, and on the other side, in the wild apple orchard that she had not visited for almost two years, she wandered about and browsed. Late in the afternoon she returned home and, coming to me, laid her head against my thigh for a moment, as if to tell me how much she had enjoyed the day. She ate all of her grain, sucked up water from her bucket, chewed briefly on her salt block, accepted from me an evening offering of apple, and settled down to sleep. Then in a night filled with furtive whisperings as the last of the leaves drifted down from the trees, she had her third and final stroke.

Squeak knew. Early in the evening he had taken only a few bites of his dinner and had left his side of the barn to go to hers, to sit just outside her door. He was there at midnight when she died, and when I went out again in the morning he was still there, dozing, head bowed so that his nose touched the ground.

He stood in the doorway and watched me lift her onto the cart. He walked close beside her as I took her to lie where I thought she would most like to be, near Samson. He paced frantically at the head of her grave while I covered it with earth and leaves. Then when I put aside the shovel and rake and sat nearby, he sank down next to me.

"That was only her shell," I told him. "We must be glad she is free."

I had forgotten his breakfast. I went into the house and warmed his milk and put it in his bowl, then when I took it out I couldn't find him, until I looked in Pixie's half of the barn where he had never been before. He was in her stall, sitting on her bed, staring into space.

What was he seeing? What was he thinking about? The summer before last? Was he lying on a rock beside me, listening to Pixie rustling through the leaves of the fallen tree, watching Pest scamper toward us to beg for her three nuts? Did he have in him a treasure box full of memories like mine?

The next day the wind changed, blowing in hard and cold from the north, and there was a smell of snow in the air. It wouldn't have been a good day, anyway, to spend in Arcadia.

We needn't go there any more.

Born and raised in Cleveland and Sandusky, Ohio, where members of her family were boat builders and fishermen, Era Zistel spent most of her earlier years on or near the waters of Lake Erie and never saw a mountain, except in pictures, until she journeyed to New York and visited the Catskills. It was love at first sight. For a number of years she and her late husband, Eric Posselt, worked as free-lance writers in Manhattan and spent their summers in the Catskills. These vacations grew longer and longer, until finally acquisition of a pair of goats provided an excuse for not returning to the city at all.

For a while Ms. Zistel was in charge of the local library in Haines Falls, in the Catskills, but most of her life has been devoted to observing animals and nature, and writing about them in a number of books and in magazines such as the *Saturday Evening Post, Audubon, Reader's Digest,* the *New York News, Kiwanis,* the now defunct *Look, Down East, Woman's Day,* and the *Defenders of Wildlife.*